Be The Voice

For Those That Are Too Broken
To Raise Their Own

THE LIFE OF
JAYANDRA

You cannot kill a body that is already dead by callous actions…
The soul will desire to escape! Death is a certainty for us all,
so why have we not mastered grief and living authentically? A
narrative that transcends beyond the shadows of suicide.

KELLY MARKEY

Bestselling and award-winning Author

Brand Ambassador: Global Movement of HOPE

Copyright © 2024 Kelly Markey

THE LIFE OF JAYANDRA

First published by Markey Writing Academy 2024

Find us on Facebook @KellyMarkeyAuthor and Instagram @Author_Kelly_Markey

Paperback ISBN: 978-0-6451968-4-9

E-Book ISBN: 978-0-6451968-5-6

Kelly Markey has asserted her rights under the Copyright, Designs and Patents Act 1988 to be identified as the author of this work. The information in this book is based on the author's experiences and opinions. The publisher specifically disclaims responsibility for any adverse consequences which may result from use of the information contained herein. Permission to use information has been sought by the author. Any breaches will be rectified in further editions of the book.

All rights reserved. No part of this publication may be reproduced, stored in or introduced into a retrieval system, or transmitted in any form, or by any means (electronic, mechanical, photocopying, recording or otherwise) without the prior written permission of the author. Any person who does any unauthorised act in relation to this publication may be liable to criminal prosecution and civil claims for damages. Enquiries should be made to the publisher.

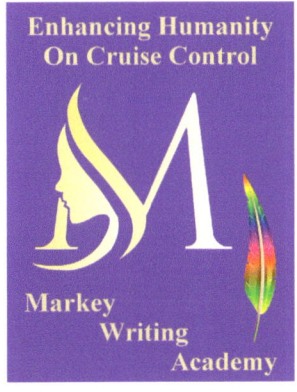

Cover Design: Markey Writing Academy

Layout: Markey Writing Academy

Typesetting: Markey Writing Academy

Cover Photograph: Taken by Kelly Markey, Australia 2016

Markey Writing Academy
Central Coast New South Wales,
Australia 2250
www.kellymarkey.com

Table of Contents

Important Contacts	2
Tributes to Jayandra	5
Kudos for the Book: Life of Jayandra	10
Foreword	13
Preface	19
Introduction	23
1. Heart to Heart Connection	28
2. Unravelling the Complexity	36
3. Human Welfare	45
Defining helplessness	51
Problem-solving abilities are affected	51
How to deal with this - My happy place	51
Frameworks for problem-solving are essential	52
4. Listening to the Silent Cry	53
5. Suicide Statistics: Let us Change the Narrative	61
How to Talk to a Suicidal Person	66
6. The Kernel of Life	70
7. Suicide Prevention in the Technology Age	77
Smoothie Recipe	85
8. Residues Before and After Suicide	86
Jayandra's Cheeky Chutney Recipe	98
9. Concepts to Transform Your Life	100
10. What Good Can Spark?	108
11. Grief and Trauma	115
Trauma	115
Grief	116
Common Grief Emotions	123

12. Afterlife and Consciousness	126
Conclusion	132
Tool 1. Tools to Navigate to a Better Season	140
Tool 2. Building Emotional Resilience and Intelligence	144
Tool 3. Living YOUR Mission	147
Tool 4. Anxiety Versus Stress	150
Tool 5. The Optimism Gallery	153
Tool 6. Mandatory Reporting	157
How to Generate Mandatory Reports	158
How to Report Suicide	159
When to Take Crucial, Immediate Action	160
Tool 7. The Dos and Don'ts of Suicide	162
Tool 8. Risk Assessment	166
Tool 9. Stop, Start and Continue Matrix	170
Tool 10. Prayer Pathway	173
Acknowledgements	178
About the Author	180
Other Books by Kelly Markey	182
What Readers Are Saying About Kelly Markey's Books	183
Magazine Appearances	184
Markey Writing Academy	185
Work with Kelly Markey	186
Featured On These Top Platforms	187
This Book Gives Hope	188
Reference	189

Kelly Markey

Thank you, Jayandra, for affording me the privilege to be a pea in a pod with you in this audacious life. Your life was always adorned with courage. The splendour of your heart did not wear pain on your sleeve. Your presence has made me a better sister, and I will forever cherish you.

Your absence has penetrated me like an arrow ripped backward from my heart. Your non-existence has changed the trajectory of my life. Life may have broken your heart, but it opened so many eyes - take that as a profound WIN my brother.

As we wonder how our feet go forward when yours cannot…

May the fishing campfire keep you warm as you rest in eternal peace, Jayandra.

To all my readers, may your decisions reflect your possibilities, not your worries. A perfected life never arrives. Life is full of seemingly infinite issues, and then LIFE ENDS. Therefore, live abundantly and authentically in the imperfect present.

"You are not the darkness you endured. You are the light that you refuse to surrender." - John Mark Green.

Important Contacts

It is essential to approach the topic of suicide with sensitivity and care. If you or a loved one is struggling with suicidal thoughts, please seek professional help immediately. Reach out to a helpline, a mental health professional, a trusted person in your life, or individuals with lived experiences.

This book aims to create awareness, provide support, and promote compassion and understanding of suicide; however, it should not be considered a substitute for professional advice or intervention. Seek professional help.

Australian support organisations – contact list:

If someone's life is in danger or there is an immediate risk of harm, call emergency services at **000.**

13YARN

13YARN is an Aboriginal and Torres Strait Islander crisis support line funded by the Australian government with the support of Lifeline and developed in collaboration with Gayaa Dhuwi (Proud Spirit) Australia.

13yarn.org.au

Contact Number (24/7) **13 92 76**

1800RESPECT

1800RESPECT is the national sexual assault, domestic, and family violence counselling service.

1800respect.org.au

Contact Number (24/7) **1800 73 77 32**

Beyond Blue

Beyond Blue provides information and support to help everyone in Australia achieve the best possible mental health, whatever their age and wherever they live.

beyondblue.org.au

Contact Number (24/7) **1300 224 636**

Lifeline

Lifeline is the national charity providing all Australians experiencing emotional distress with access to 24-hour crisis support and suicide prevention services.

Lifeline.org.au

Contact Number (24/7) **13 11 14**

No To Violence

Counselling for men who have anger, relationship, or parenting issues.

ntv.org.au

Contact Number (24/7) **1300 766 491**

Qlife

QLife provides Australia-wide anonymous, LGBTIQ+ peer support and referral for people wanting to talk about a range of issues, including sexuality, identity, gender, bodies, feelings, or relationships.

qlife.org.au

Contact Number (24/7) **1800 184 527**

Suicide Call Back Service

Counselling for suicide prevention and mental health via telephone, online, and video for anyone affected by suicide doors.

suicidecallbackservice.org.au

Contact Number (24/7) **1300 659 467**

South African support organisations – contact list:

South African Depression and Anxiety Group (SADAG)

Helpline: 0800 567 567

Website: www.sadag.org

Lifeline South Africa

Helpline: 0861 322 322 (24/7)

Website: www.lifelinesa.co.za

Suicide Crisis Helpline

(Cipla 24hr Mental Health Helpline)

Helpline: 0800 456 789 (24/7)

Website: www.cipla24.co.za

Please get in touch with these helplines or seek assistance from mental health professionals who can provide the support and guidance you or your loved ones need. Remember, you are not alone; some people care and want to help.

Tributes to Jayandra

My loving son, as I sit here to pen down these words, my heart overflows with love and sorrow. You came into this world, bringing a joy that touched everyone around you. You were a beacon of light, a soul so pure, intelligent, and gentle, and you brought happiness to all who knew you. Your smile could brighten the darkest days, and your laughter echoed like a melody in our hearts. As you grew, you showed us what it meant to be compassionate and caring. You had an uncanny ability to understand others' feelings and offer comfort without hesitation. Your kindness and generosity knew no bounds, and you taught me the true meaning of selflessness. Your unreserved love for all the children in the neighbourhood—buying them chips and sweets—has left a massive gap in many hearts. Jayandra, you will never be forgotten. Your legacy of love and kindness will continue to ripple through the lives of those you touched. Rest now, my precious son, in eternal peace. Until we meet again, know that you will always be cherished, loved, and missed.

Jaimathee Ramlucken: Mum, Mandeni, South Africa.

Seconds turned into years of happiness, sadness, joy, laughter, pain, and sorrow. The memories my family and I shared with you will always be a privilege, and I will forever cherish every moment. The love, compassion, and care you bestowed on my children never went unnoticed, and I salute you for loving them unconditionally. You will always be remembered and loved fondly.

Aruna Ramlucken: Aunty, Pietermaritzburg, South Africa.

My loving nephew, Jayandra, had a heart of gold. You had an amazing helping hand, even though your hand was disabled. You invited us for your 50th birthday, but instead, it was your funeral. You left without saying goodbye, and we never really got to celebrate you. I will forever remember all the good old memories. You are now in wholesome hands, and we pray that you watch over and protect us, especially your mum, who mourns you every day. I love you, stacks. Rest in peace, until we meet again.

Rajesh Ramlucken: Uncle, Richards Bay, South Africa.

As I sit here, overwhelmed with grief, I find solace in the cherished memories we shared. You were not just a brother to me; you were a confidant, a friend, and a guiding light in my life. Your untimely departure has left an emptiness in my heart that words can scarcely describe. From the moment we were born, our lives were intertwined, and we grew up together, sharing laughter, secrets, and dreams. You had a unique way of brightening every room you entered, and your infectious laughter could lift the heaviest of hearts. Your vibrant spirit and warm smile drew people to you like moths to a flame. You were an adventurer at heart, always seeking new experiences and embracing life's challenges enthusiastically. Your determination and courage inspired us all, reminding us to face our obstacles with a brave spirit. The memories we created together are etched in my mind and soul forever. From our first game to our memories and the countless moments we shared as a family - each memory is a treasure I hold close to my heart. My love for you will always burn bright.

Ishwar Rampershad: Brother, Mandeni, South Africa.

To my nephew, Jayandra: We must accept that you are forever gone, but we will keep you alive in our hearts and homes. Your loss has hit us all so hard. I knew you to be such a compassionate, loving and humble person. You always looked out for others first. My sons and husband will miss the fishing trips, and we will forever cherish our time with you. Your kindness and generosity were much appreciated by all. The beautiful memories you left behind will never fade away. You left without saying goodbye. I will miss you being around, and I hope you are at peace now and know I will see you again - love, your aunt, forever and always.

Sharm Duwarka: Aunty, Richards Bay, South Africa.

To my cousin, brother, Jayandra: death leaves a heartache no one can heal, and love leaves a memory no one can steal. I still cannot bear the reality that you are no longer with us. Thank you for the unforgettable memories that we shared. Your visits to my home will forever be cherished. You brought so much joy and happiness to my younger daughter. You were the first cousin that my little one had a bond with. You had a heart that cared completely and a smile that brought so much pleasure. Your humbleness and kindness will live forever in our hearts. You are gone but never forgotten. Rest in peace. Until we meet again, lots of love.

Vash Ramiah: Cousin, Empangeni, South Africa.

You had a passion for life that was infectious. Your enthusiasm for your interests and hobbies was contagious, inspiring others to follow their passions with the same fervour. Your absence leaves a void that cannot be filled, but your spirit will forever live on in the hearts of those you touched.

Though your time with us was cut short, your impact will resonate for eternity. You have left an indelible mark on my life, and I promise to honour your memory by carrying forth the lessons you taught me—to love fiercely, to cherish every moment, to give selflessly to others, and to be an authentic friend regardless of circumstances.

David Juste: Friend, Mauritius.

Your passing has left an emptiness that words can never fully express. Yet, amidst the grief, I am grateful for our time together. You enriched my life beyond measure, and I am blessed to call you, my brother. Though you are no longer physically present, your spirit lives on within each of us who love you. You will forever be the guiding star that leads us through the darkest nights, and your memory will fuel our strength in times of weakness.

Shammy Rampershad: Sister, Mandeni, South Africa.

The first time I met Jay, I was blown away by how much of an easy-going guy he was, and because of this, there was an instant connection between us. We only spent a few days together each time, but we got on like a house on fire. I would say if we lived in the same location, then we would have been best friends. I am one hundred per cent sure of this. It was amazing to meet another person I did not spend that much time with but had a connection with. Jay made me feel like I had known him forever. Rest in peace, Jay, and we will catch up again, my brother.

Simon James: Friend, Queensland, Australia.

As I bid you farewell, I find comfort in knowing that you are at peace, watching over us from above. Until we meet again, dear friend, rest easy in the embrace of eternity. You will always be loved, remembered, and deeply missed. You created an impression I will forever carry in my heart: you showed up for life even in the difficult seasons. I am sorry that the load got so heavy for you eventually. Love forever.

Kenny Juste: Friend, Netherlands.

I remember when I first met Jay back in 2016, we got on instantly. He was a great bloke who did not talk much but was always a great company and a genuinely good guy. We hung out quite a bit when he was in Australia, and we always shared a laugh and a few beers. It was great to meet someone from halfway across the world and feel akin to him. He will be sorely missed. We are all saddened, and those who knew him will never forget him.

Ross Haydon: Friend, Sydney, Australia.

Jayandra, you were a source of inspiration to all who knew you. Your relentless determination and unwavering optimism taught me that no challenge was insurmountable and that the power of hope could overcome any adversity. You faced life with courage and grace, even in the darkest times. Your compassion knew no bounds. I witnessed countless acts of kindness as you selflessly helped those in need without seeking recognition or reward. Your generosity touched the lives of so many, and your impact on this world is immeasurable. Even though physical distance rarely united us, I grew up to realise that you had a beautiful name and were a gem. I recall family gatherings and sleepovers where you remained humble and polite regardless of intoxication. You were extremely responsible and helpful. Even with your disabled hand, you ensured everything was cleaned and packed before and after our braai or gathering. I recall your compassion for my welfare to keep warm in the winter. As cousins, we shared a bond that extended beyond blood. We were partners in mischief and adventure, creating memories I will forever hold dear. Our late-night talks about life, love, and everything in between were moments of genuine connection that I will always treasure.

Aruna Roopanand: Cousin, Port Shepstone, South Africa.

My dearest friend, Jayandra, I can still hear your voice. At first, it brought sorrow, and then it brought anger. These feelings emerged from a cohort of people who should have cared for you but did not. My dearest friend Jayandra, I can still hear your expression; it brings joy and cheers because that is who you are. I will never forget your role for my grandchildren, husband, and myself. My dearest friend Jayandra, I can still hear your declaration, and it now echoes in concert with a million other voices. Encouraging us all to speak up about human welfare and not allow others to bully people into suicide with any candour.

Peggy Imbrailo: Neighbour / Friend, Mandeni, South Africa.

I briefly knew Jayandra; it was enough to know his heart was one of genuineness and tenderness. He was easy to get to know, with only a precious few of whom undertook the effort to do so. He truly knew the value of the gifts given to him. He had modest means and modest needs. A meaningful conversation was enough to brighten his whole day. I enjoyed our time together fishing, talking of past tales, past catches, and ones that got away. He had great knowledge of this, his favourite pass-time, and was eager to pass his knowledge on to whoever was interested. He was a patient and good instructor. May your soul rest in peace, dear Jayandra.

You are and will always be missed by those you have touched profoundly. Many cared for you more than you ever knew.

Dave Markey: Brother-in-Law, Sydney, Australia.

Sometimes, we wander from place to place in quest for a diamond, but it is right in the palm of your hand. Look closer, love better, and listen more. Jayandra was the gem that we let slip away. He adjusted his life to be absent rather than changing his boundaries to accommodate disrespect.

Kelly Markey: Sister, Sydney, Australia.

Never lost

Have you ever lost someone that you love?
Just hoped they were looking down from above?
Have you ever asked them for a little sign?
A symbol, a picture, any song or rhyme?

Have you ever closed your eyes and imagined them here?
Then opened them and felt them to be near?
Have you ever cried tears that they could not see?
But hoped that they'd know it's with them you'd rather be?

Have you ever lost someone that you love?
Just hoped they could see your smile from above?
Knowing that they are in your heart
Because it's in your memories that you are never apart.

Poem by Jacqueline Wright, Poet, Sydney, Australia.

"Birds born in a cage think flying is an illness." - Alejandro Jodorowsky.

Kudos for the Book: Life of Jayandra

In *"The Life of Jayandra,"* author Kelly explores the human spirit's resilience in the face of the unimaginable. From the lens of a devoted sister who lost her brother to the profound darkness of suicide, this book not only unravels the deeply personal experience of grief but also emerges as a vital guide for those navigating the complex labyrinth of emotions after such a loss.

As a mental health social worker, I find this book to be an invaluable resource for individuals grappling with the aftermath of suicide. The author skillfully weaves her narrative with a profound understanding of the multifaceted aspects of mental health, creating a tapestry that resonates with authenticity and empathy. *"The Life of Jayandra"* is not merely a chronicle of pain but a testament to the power of resilience and the human capacity to find hope amidst the darkest moments.

One of the commendable aspects of this book is its ability to serve as a wellspring of soothing resources for those who have lost a loved one to suicide and those who are grappling with suicidal thoughts. From the author's raw and honest reflections on her journey to coping mechanisms and support networks, readers are gently guided through the healing process. In a world where mental health is often stigmatized, this book bravely opens the door to conversations that are essential for fostering understanding and empathy.

The author's exploration of the importance of looking after one's mental health is a beacon of wisdom in a society that often neglects this critical aspect of well-being. Through the lens of personal tragedy, she advocates for a compassionate and open dialogue surrounding mental health issues. This book is a powerful reminder that we must prioritize our mental well-being and foster environments that encourage seeking help without judgement.

Above all, *"The Life of Jayandra"* encourages readers to live with hope. It is a testament to the strength of embracing vulnerability and seeking support. As a mental health professional, I appreciate the author's nuanced approach in highlighting the importance of understanding, acceptance, and the transformative power of hope in the face of despair.

In conclusion, *"The Life of Jayandra"* is a remarkable literary contribution that transcends the boundaries of grief, offering solace and guidance to those who have lost a loved one to suicide and those contemplating suicide. It is a call to action for society to prioritize mental health and create spaces where individuals can find understanding, support, and, most importantly, hope. This book stands as a beacon of light, reminding us all that even in the darkest moments, there is the potential for healing and renewal.

Azita Abdollahian
Clinical Mental Health Social Work, Sydney, Australia.

When a loved one commits suicide, it is never an easy conversation to have. There are always so many questions left unsaid, so much grief, a void, a hole, shame, and so many different emotions one goes through, and yet so many have had to endure this tragedy one way or another and still find it hard to discuss. "The Life of Jayandra - A Narrative That Transcends Beyond the Shadows of Suicide" is a heroic personal guide from Markey that allows readers to be vulnerable enough to feel and deal with the devastating effects suicide brings with it. Markey created this book so eloquently and compassionately and allows a safe space for the reader where it is OK not to be OK. This book is undoubtedly a resilient guide for anyone seeking healing, education, understanding, and help. It is such an essential piece for all of humanity, no matter where you are in this world, because suicide does not discriminate, and you never know when you may be able to prevent it and save a life. Thank you, Mrs. Markey, for this brilliant, courageous book, and may God bless you always.

Stephanie Cirami
President, The International Association of Top Professionals, New York, United States of America.

"The Life of Jayandra: A Narrative That Transcends Beyond the Shadows of Suicide" is a masterpiece of empathy, education, and empowerment. Markey's compassionate approach and unwavering commitment to this critical topic will undoubtedly leave an indelible mark on human welfare. This book is an indispensable resource for anyone seeking to understand, prevent, and ultimately overcome the devastating impact of suicide.

Suicide Prevention, Australia.

This book, *"The Life of Jayandra,"* bridges the darkness of despair and the light of resilience, guiding readers towards a place of strength and renewed purpose. In these pages, Kelly Markey sheds light on the vital importance of community, destigmatizing human welfare struggles, and fostering a culture of open dialogue. The book serves as a rallying call to collectively address the pervasive issue of suicide, offering readers a renewed sense of urgency and the understanding that they have the power to make a difference. Accolades, passion, and thriving purpose have marked Kelly's formidable presence in the author industry. This book is a gigantic leap for humanity to quell the agony of suicide.

CBS News, United States of America.

With unwavering dedication, Kelly Markey delves into the complex and sensitive subject of suicide prevention, offering invaluable insights, practical strategies, and optimism for individuals, families, and communities grappling with this pressing issue. This book stands as a testament to Kelly's deep understanding of the intricacies surrounding suicide, human welfare, and the human experience. The author's empathetic narrative style creates an immediate connection with readers, fostering a sense of camaraderie and understanding. As readers embark on this transformative journey, they are met with a wealth of knowledge that empowers them to recognize warning signs, engage in crucial conversations, and extend a lifeline to those in need. *"The Life of Jayandra"* is more than a book; it is a lifeline. Kelly Markey provides a comprehensive toolkit of evidence-based practices, compassionate communication techniques, and real-life stories that serve as beacons of hope.

Fox News, United States of America.

As usual, Kelly brings another brilliant book to life and then some. The barbed topic does not limit her in any way, shape, or form. The daughter of the African soil sheds light on the all-important subject of suicide. This author has excellent authority to address this through her lived experience. Every reader will come out equipped and beaming to be a river of life rather than a stagnant reservoir. Kelly's connection to the reader is out of the question; this book is an engaging page-turner.

Radio host: New York, United States of America.

"The day you plant the seed is not the day you eat the fruit; remember to plant strategically in life." - Kelly Markey.

Foreword

Nadene Joy is a global advisor, leadership strategist, philanthropist, and world-class changemaker passionate about bringing greater hope, love, faith, peace, purpose, healing, and joy into the world one person at a time. She is a Board Director and advisor to many non-profit organizations in her local community and across the globe, and she has recently been given the prestigious Woman of Heart and Visionary of Hope Award and the 2023 BIZZ Business Excellence Award for being a successful leader who has consistently demonstrated business excellence. She has worked alongside some of the most influential leaders of our time, including Joe Foster, founder of REEBOK. She has been featured in numerous top media outfits, such as USA TODAY and many others globally. She is devoted to bringing greater mental health awareness, being the voice for the vulnerable in society, supporting men, women, and children's programs, empowering communities through access to education and uplifting the lives of all others she encounters.

Words cannot begin to express my undying gratitude and thanks to trailblazer Kelly Markey for the most incredible honour and opportunity to deliver this foreword of the magnificent writings of authentic truth to the world. When we gather to support and unconditionally love one another just as we are with no strings attached, we recognize the sheer importance of "unity in community." May you learn through the innate wisdom, stories, and teachings of this book that we are all a part of something so much greater than ourselves, a greater purpose, so to speak and that each one of us has a unique purpose on Earth to bring greater love and light to the planet during a time in history where there is such darkness and chaos everywhere we look and turn in society. Our sense of belongingness to a group, to a greater community, and to serve and do good for others, even by being a part of and having the prestigious opportunity to read and immerse yourself in this extraordinary publication, is a gift. Did you know that our sense of belongingness is a core basic need of human survival and is next in importance alongside having food, shelter, and clothing?

There are no coincidences in life. You are here today reading this for a reason and a greater purpose that perhaps you don't quite understand yet. Everything happens for a reason, including meeting the people you need to meet to assist and elevate you or teach you lessons for your healing journey of becoming the best, most integral version of yourself that you can be. You are my mirror, and I am yours. Think about one person you genuinely admire most in this world, and then think about the top three character traits you love most about them. Now, get a pen and paper and write them down.

Take a moment to look at these characteristics and know that what you see and admire in others is also inside of you. Many of us have not unlocked or accessed those traits or gifts yet, as too much other stuff is blocking and clouding our perceptions and vision to recognize them. We must begin to acknowledge that no one is perfect and have this awareness first to realise that we need to start to heal our own negative limiting beliefs and less-than-ideal circumstances from childhood and our lives. We must move from the dark to the light and know there is hope today. Realise you do not have to wait until tomorrow to have hope. It comes from your intrinsic choice to move forward towards the light right now, in this exact moment. Let us redefine the perception of what society says is "hope for tomorrow" and replace it with "hope for today" through a term I have personally coined as "actionable hope."

"People will never rise above their own opinions of themselves." If you believe you are not good enough or worthy of great things, this will be your reality. When we step back to take an honest look through the unconditional loving eyes of God, we will begin to see the roots of what caused the lies and negative beliefs about who we are that is not our truth. Society brings us down and makes us feel inferior, but God, on the other hand, is an all-encompassing God who takes the dark and moves it into the light from the root and heals all our wounds one step at a time. No matter what you are currently going through in your journey through life, know that you are exactly where you are meant to be to learn what you need to. God is diligently preparing you for your life's next stage and journey. Our job is to trust and surrender to God's greater plan and purpose, not only for our entire lives but just starting today. What is your purpose for today? I encourage you to sit silently in prayer, gratitude, and meditation, and ask God what your purpose is today. And then wait in silence until the answer is revealed. We all have a purpose in life, but we do not have to think we have to have our entire lives figured out just for us today, in this present moment. Forget about the past; there is nothing you can do now to change what happened. This is where depression lives. And stop worrying about what may or may not occur as it has not happened yet. This is where we feel anxious and unsettled. The only thing you can truly control is this exact moment, the present moment. That is why it is called the "present" moment, as it is the most significant "gift" we could give ourselves and all others we encounter. This is where authentic, eternal peace lives in our souls. Trust God's plan over your expectations and outcomes of how you think it should be, and know his plan is always perfect.

Trust, surrender, and then repeat. Let go and let God. Your life is God's gift to you and the world—how you choose to live your life is your gift to God. When you contemplate suicide, it is like completely disrespecting God, as He is the one who has graciously given you the precious gift of life. It is a pain we all go through, and when the pain gets too much, I challenge you to begin to look in the now, in this exact present moment, at your unique purpose in life and turn "your pain into purpose."

Did you know that, on average, statistics show there are approximately 130 suicides per day and that in 2021, men died by suicide 3.90 times more than women? We need to pay attention to this and take action to support our fellow citizens currently suffering in silence. We must authentically talk about issues that truly matter as they save lives.

There is not one person on the planet who has not gone through pain or felt like giving up on something at some point throughout their life. We all have suffered varying degrees of pain, have suffered from broken hearts and disappointments, have experienced depression and/or anxiety, or have felt overwhelmed and have needed someone to pray for us during these times to know we are not alone. Do not ever think it is weak to ask someone for help and be persistent. Do not give up until you get the help that is needed and required. Did you also know that personality matters? The extroverted person, for example, sees the world as a "social opportunity," and the introvert sees the world as a place to retreat from and spend time alone—in fact, both are ideal, but only if you are fortunate enough to match your temperament and personality with your environment. The environment and who you surround yourself with matter. Did you know you are the sum of the top five people you spend the most time with? Choose your friends wisely; it is time to seriously reconsider them as a part of your trusted inner circle and a tribe of supporters.

The Tree Foundation of Hope

A tree is a powerful symbol of hope. **"If a tree is cut down, there is hope that it will grow again and send out new branches**." Even if its deep roots grow old in the ground, and its stump dies in the dirt, at the onset of water, it will bud out new shoots and life. Hope is like the tree of life; even where life fails to appear to exist, hope endures with possibility and is the light in the darkness. It comes as no surprise, then, that in the face of tragedies of life, trees often become symbols of strength, resilience, perseverance, and deep hope. "**When we see a tree come back from the brink of destruction, it inspires us and reminds us that life goes on and we can and will find a way to heal and grow**."

Trees, along with hope, help us become more aware of our connections with something much larger than ourselves. Hope is a gift that works together to give us confidence, joy, peace, power, and love. We risk descending into despair without hope and other virtues such as faith and unconditional love.

Hope, with faith and trust, gives us motivation and coupled with action, plays a vital role in moving us towards achieving our goals.

"Hope without action is like fire without fuel." - Nadene Joy

We can hope for something all day long; however, if we do not choose to "do" something about it to make a change and take action, nothing will change, and we will continue to stay in the same cycle and situation we have been in for months or even perhaps our entire life. Action fuels hope just as wood fuels fire.

The Tree of Life also synchronistically symbolizes one's unique individuality. Trees, like each one of us and like our fingerprints, are all unique, with their branches sprouting at different points and, most times, in completely different directions. It symbolizes a person›s growth into a unique human being as different experiences shape us into who we are today. Remember to always honour yourself wherever you are on your journey and remember that you will never be given anything too big to handle. Be patient and hopeful, as anything is possible when you have faith and believe in it. With God, all things are possible. *"Someone will be attracted to your light; others will fear it. Decide to shine anyway." – unknown.*

Every person in the world should live with hope, the light from within us all. Everyone must go through difficult enduring tests at different times in life, and hope, along with a daily purpose, is the only thing that helps us get good results in those tests and learn the lessons required for our individual growth to prepare us for what adventure in life is next to come. Remain optimistic no matter what, as there will always be peaks and valleys; this is life. It is how you respond with love and grace and not just react out of old habits and patterns that matter most, leading to greater awareness to consciously take action to begin doing something different than you previously did.

No matter how you look at it, the world has no substitute for hope.

Breaking the Silence, There is Hope: Men Matter.

In my professional opinion, there is much more that needs to be done in our collective world, as there are countless men and families who love them who have yet to realize their "Infinite Worth."

It is time now to begin to think about taking radical action to unite professionals, family, and friends across the globe to provide the safe place required for good men to break their suffering in silence and heal. The darkness of depression and suicidal ideation is very real, but there is hope to move from the dark to the light and take up the cause to normalize this predominant narrative.

If you have ever experienced trauma as a form of abuse or even a loss, you might have felt it is your fault. Children especially often blame themselves when they have no other way to cope with the pain of their external surroundings. Did you know that men tend to keep their childhood trauma a secret for an average of 24 years, as they do not want to burden another person with the pain of the experience? Did you know that so many men you perceive to be influencers, successful industry leaders, pro athletes, or artists excruciatingly suffer in silence every day? The emotions that define us and the patterns that limit us are embedded in trauma and must be released before we can heal. You might have heard the saying and general rule that people who mistreat other people more often than not also mistreat themselves. Therefore, it is more important to break the generational cycle of suffering in silence (and also its connection to trauma/abuse) that exists across the board globally. Predominantly in men (but also in women.)

For us to come together in unity with one another, even to reach millions of men with this imperative message, we must first begin to address the deeper "root cause" in all aspects and encourage men of all ages to speak up and seek help. It can be, and in fact, it is that simple. Start today to break the silence by sharing with just one person you love and trust and with one person who is a trained professional in healing trauma.

Please know that asking for help shows your innate strength and is not a sign of weakness. Make sure you take action to reach out for help in some way, any way you can, as it has the potential to save your life.

There are many men you might know right now who suffer silently with hidden secrets of childhood trauma. Never forget that it takes men 24 years to reveal their secrets. That is 24 years on average that they carry this pain, feelings of guilt, shame, fear, self-doubt, anger, sadness, and overall lack of self-worth, and they live well below their true potential in life as many are limited by their past.

Our goal is to continue to love and support others, knowing that none of us is perfect and that men are truly doing the best they can. We all strive to be good people and men and women who live honourably, integrally, and intentionally. Act and show up with purpose; each morning, when you get out of bed, cultivate a greater purpose for the day ahead.

Know that it is OK to be real, vulnerable, safe, supported, and authentic, especially with other men. This is necessary to heal and move forward with greater freedom and faith—to leave our burdens and pain behind and let God carry them for you. All men and women alike need to know they are safe when they break their silence. Healing can take place at any time we choose and does not have to start when we get to rock bottom. Let us take preventive action and have greater hope today, knowing we can begin our healing today. The day our secrets are no longer hidden, and our healing begins, infinite possibilities in the universe will open up as our lives become instantaneously better. The countless opportunities we have dreamed of for our entire lives reveal themselves, and slowly, doors are opened beyond our wildest dreams. Our relationships improve, and we begin to fully realize our self-imposed limits are gone and believe in our value and worth in the world.

Good people support other people, and good men help other men. They teach, guide, support, and mentor them. They unite with them in the community and most importantly, provide a sense of deep trust and love without conditions or any strings attached.

Together, we can make a positive difference that will change the lives of men, their families, and generations to follow. Always continue to choose loving kindness for yourself and others over hate, to shine brightly, to share your gifts and talents with others, and to help bring greater kindness, love, and hope to at least ONE person every day, as the world needs YOU now more than ever before in history. Your smile matters. You matter. You belong here. You are loved beyond measure. We bring eternal HOPE to others when we help other people elevate and rise today through our actions, our listening, and the time we spend with them, letting them know they truly matter and that they are fully seen, valued, and heard in each moment and this world.

Together, we are much stronger in unity as a part of a greater conscious community than we are apart. Trust in the Lord with all your heart, and do not lean on your understanding. In all your ways, acknowledge him, and he will make straight your paths. (Proverbs 3:5-6). For I know the plans I have for you, declares the Lord, plans for welfare and not for evil, to give you a future and hope. (Jeremiah 29:11).

To Your Success with Love,

Nadene Joy
CEO of Nadene Joy Consulting Inc.
www.NadeneJoy.com
Canada

"How vain it is to sit down and write when you have not stood up to live." - Henry David Thoreau.

Preface

I am sincerely sorry that you are embarking on a journey to learn about suicide. It is essential to approach this topic with sensitivity and respect for all individuals involved. Regardless of whether you are contemplating suicide, impacted by suicide, or a support worker for suicide prevention, this is a crucial panorama for humanity. I am also elated that you took the plunge to equip yourself on this profound topic that is part and parcel of our global landscape.

My life as an international bestselling author began increasing the possibility quotient when I was nominated as a finalist for the Woman Changing the World Awards in 2023. I sojourned to London for the award celebration. I continued the daily ritual of calling my mum in South Africa, and on three occasions, I did a video call, which my brother Jayandra answered.

With his prelude of squealing with delight as he planned his 50th birthday bash, he was suddenly lost in his celebration lustre. I was delighted to see him looking forward to his milestone. He looked me in the eyes and thanked me for his birthday gift. Drinking in the droplets of time in retrospection, I wondered what I could have said if I had known these were my last conversations with him.

I was in transit on my return flight from London, with a stop-over in Los Angeles, making our way to our connecting flight to Sydney. Suddenly, my Marino cardigan felt claustrophobic, and I needed to rip it off. I did not quite feel myself even after I removed it. I drank water and told my husband, Dave, that I needed to sit. I felt awash and could not get back up on my feet, so I sat there to catch my breath. With my persistent angst, I focused on gaining composure, and then I grabbed my phone to connect to the Wi-Fi and the online world.

BOOM!

This was not what I had expected in my wildest dreams; my phone chimed with numerous messages. Messages of condolences! It was a vortex; initially, I thought it was a joke, then I reasoned it was a bad dream, and finally, I looked at Dave and asked him if this was real. Productive paranoia set in, and then reality came knocking again. I could not breathe properly and had one more flight to reach home, Sydney. Acquiring befitting composure, I called South Africa, and it was confirmed that I was not dreaming. My brother passed on. A reality that was irrational in a very predictable way. Delusions masqueraded as impossibilities in my fluctuating mind. I calmed myself and called my mum again, informing her I was boarding my flight and would be offline. Sadly, yes, indeed, she was still in mourning.

I had to strap myself into a seat of silence on a flight that seemed to take forever when all I felt was bedlam. I disembarked the flight feeling sick as a dog. With a gnawing sense of vulnerability, rancour, and anger all rolled into one. I tested positive for COVID-19, we were relocating, and now I had an international funeral.

I watched my brother's funeral on livestream while in quarantine. There was not a soul to console me. It was the hardest event in my life. The camera guy did not zoom in on my brother's face, and I only wanted to look at his face one last time. They were moving to shut the coffin, and I was calling everyone from Australia to ask them to let me look at his face. No one had their phones with them. It is a mammoth effort to chisel into the death of a sibling all by oneself in a foreign country and now in isolation. I watched the stream on replay all night until I could cry no more.

His eulogy had two vague lines about his character. This is when I knew I had to write a book about the life of Jayandra, who he was and his authentic character - what his life represented and the legacy that he left behind.

Jayandra was poised between modest and caring attributes, weaving repartee into everyday life. Je ne sais quoi is often used as praise for someone's attractiveness, style, or charisma. It is a French expression that means, "I don't know what," and it is used to describe those intangible qualities that make someone special or unique. Tears well up as I gather my thoughts to describe my brother's intangible qualities. I have no actual words, but this French expression brings me close. He was free in his wilderness; he was a wanderer of the ocean that belonged to no man, woman, or city. Jayandra brought passion to all that he did, especially his fishing expeditions. He hooked some of the biggest fish in the country. He dressed his best and dined on deliciousness. He made simple pleasure a priority. He was a sauntered man who took his time to savour the moment. He lived within the mystery of watching movies and documentaries. He was playful, compassionate, and caring, filled with wit that exploded at the most unexpected times. The fire of Ramlucken roared in him, and the fishermen's DNA pumped into his veins. His genius belonged to his cluster, which knew him as a remarkable fisherman steeped in adventure. Adept at navigating life despite the arduous.

When a horse breaks its leg, it is put out of its misery because it will never heal correctly. Jayandra's spirit was broken and tormented. May the rich blessings of forgiveness permeate his soul and may the virtues of the Lord lead him to heaven. When the dust settles, what matters is the life you lived with the time that was bestowed upon you.

If you want to see the true measure of a man, watch how he treats his inferiors, not his equals. I paid attention to how people treated Jayandra during his life and after his death.

Human diaspora, despair, self-destruction, dysfunction, loss, victory, achievements, and triumphs are telling signs. Intellectual loyalty means defending strong convictions. Intellectual integrity is being convinced by strong arguments. A key to growth is being willing to change what is wrong. You miss out on opportunities when you only ask what could go wrong. It is also worth asking what could go right. Change comes with the inherent risk that you may fail. However, sticking to the status quo also comes with the risk that we may fail to grow.

No heart can forget a sibling that you loved. No one can mentor you to deal with the pain of never having the opportunity to say goodbye. This pain is unique for everyone. Time most certainly does not heal all of us. Reminisced and remembered, but never eliminated. It is okay to have your heart shattered into a million pieces and ache for your loved one scattered on the ground as the world moves on swiftly. As you journey through this milestone, each piece of memory stored in your heart will unravel new revelations and create a balm to heal your soul. As I navigated through this vortex, I also discovered who was concerned about my welfare. This is a beautiful message from a friend:

"Hi Kelly, just writing to see how you are doing. You have been on my mind, and I hope that the pain and shock of losing your wonderful, sweet brother is getting a little easier to bear. I'm so sorry you are going through this when all the other exciting things are happening in your life. You worked hard to be where you are, and I wish you so much strength as you go through all these emotions. I know that you are a strong Tugela girl, but you need to have yourself in one of those crying sessions that brings all that pain out. Don't keep it inside because you need to be free of such hurt and pain. I'm certain that your brother knew how much you cared and loved him, but sometimes those who take their life are in so much pain that love cannot even reach them. It's never a shortcoming of yours, so never blame yourself for what had to be, to end their pain.

I know this because my dad also killed himself, and we had to grapple with all the things that we could have done to save him from himself, but you can't, and my dad was 48 when he died, so it hurts to know that there were so many more years to enjoy together. But living is hard when your heart believes the world will be better without you. I'm so sorry that your brother was lost in this untruth; I pray that he will always be your guiding light when times are hard for you. I always remember my sweet, handsome dad for the good person he was, and I take comfort in knowing he is in a better place waiting to see us again. Memories may fade, but the heart never forgets. I know God holds you in his hands even when the pain is unbearable. I send you warm hugs and so much strength to make sense of all this, and I hope you will remember to let me know when you are in the US again to get that great big 'hug' in person. You can always call me if you need to talk. Anytime, I'm always here."

It was so refreshing to receive this note, yet most people have no concept of how to reach out, while others take it to the next level. For your welfare, ensure that you have a circle that will support you in every season of life. Global bestselling and award-winning author Kelly Markey takes you through her lived experience via the shadows of suicide, and she shines a light on prevention. This narrative also blows the whistle on the signs. Urging humanity to work in concert with each other to break the silence of suicide. This is a deeply personal tribute to her brother, Jayandra, who is sadly part of the suicide statistics. He navigated through disability, lack of visibility, and extortion from so-called loved ones. This journey highlights the remnants after a loved one ends his life. This book will shine a light on suicide and show you how to embrace hope and resilience, inspire change, reflect on the journey of suicide, encourage a collective effort to prevent suicide, improve human welfare, and thus create a brighter future for all.

You can never win by playing dirty. Karma is real. You reap what you sow. What goes around comes around - Lessons Taught by Life.

Introduction

Life is full of revelations: when your day is magnificent, appreciate it. When it becomes challenging, remain resilient. There are no guarantees on how many days you have left, so be grateful for each minute. From all the roads that Jayandra travelled, the journey back to himself was the most magnificent to live in peace with his portion of life. He craved for nothing but a simple life. Death will not hold you back from changing the world, brother. This book is a tribute to a life gone too soon. It was tragic to perform his last rites on his 50th birthday. There was no party, not even a celebration of his life. Suicide unleashes trauma like no other.

The **truth** does not mind being questioned. **A lie** does not like being challenged. Most that purported support for the grieving in society fluctuated like the wind in all earnest. Remorse and apology are sobering; when you are genuinely sorry, you will lose grandiosity and superiority. You will zoom in and admit your wrongdoings. It is a surrender that brings an equalizer to an unbalanced equation. It is embarking on a true, authentic connection with yourself and those you have wronged. Remorse and apology are remembering and acknowledging that what you conspired to do occurred. Some characters live in a world that fuels them to cheat, lie, and kill. They will never see the light, change their wicked ways, or simply apologise. You do not require an apology to heal. Excavate the pain endured and seek the path to your healing. It is not human to simply move on after the suicide of a loved one. Trauma responses are normal; seek healing to adjust to a new life and how you want to move forward.

Never be naïve and pretend evil does not exist. Always recognise its existence, but never its authority. You did not just wake up and become a butterfly; growth is a process. You **CAN** avoid reality, but you **CANNOT** prevent the consequences of avoiding reality. Stop lying to intuitive people. You are embarrassing yourself. Trust is earned, respect is given, and loyalty is demonstrated. The betrayal of any one of these is to lose three. You are weak when your experience causes someone to create a noose and hang themselves. When something terrible happens, you have three choices. You can either let it define you, destroy you, or strengthen you for a greater comeback. We are all the same: at some point, broken, then put back together, more beautiful than before because we persevered.

The world you see is created by what you focus on. It is never too late to adjust your lens. You can look at each day as an obstacle or as an opportunity. The best outfit is self-respect. Do not lose it. Naturally, we all show symptoms of despair after a suicide. It was sad to see people use

Jayandra when he was alive, and even when he was dead, they had no respect for him, his character, or the memories they were destroying. They continued to lie and make up stories, even after an innocent person was dead. From the little that he had, people were around him like hyenas asking for help. He trusted the beggar like his brother and opened his heart and wallet. The hand that fed was bitten. It was so bitten that it was traumatised for almost two years.

Jayandra sent a text message with a picture of a noose with the caption, *"You are pushing me to suicide,"* a year before he killed himself. I am still grappling with what the greater tragedy is! From the little that he had, he chose to help his so-called relative. However, his relative showed no concern or compassion for his plight. For a significant part of my life, I believed I never did enough, but I was doing far too much. It was just for the wrong people. Sadly, Jayandra found himself on the loaded end of this equation, which overwhelmed him. Wherewithal is the only motto that some people live by. Granted that he appeared to be a docile character, they took advantage of him and did not care about the alarming scream for help. It breaks my heart to have witnessed how well Jayandra lived out this scripture, yet no one could return the favour. ***"Some friendships do not last, but some friends are more loyal than brothers." - Proverbs 18:24.***

Many have fallen into maladaptive traps, and there is no comeback. For those readers who are struck in the valley of despair right now, do not let the entire staircase overwhelm you. Just focus on the first step. Make your future vision so clear that the immediate setback becomes irrelevant. The most prominent person in your life is you. Stop acting like you are afraid of your power. Stop believing that nothing is too good for you. Trust yourself at this moment to take yourself where you need to be. Challenges are gifts that force us to search for a new centre of gravity. Never fight them; find a new way to stand. Luck is a myth. Determination fights off doubts and invests in a better future. Craft your ability to see the benefit and blessing in every setback; this is a mandatory life skill. Never dim your light to make others more comfortable. Let yourself shine, and they can squint! Find the strength to request that others remove their foot from your mood and throat.

Always remember that you are measurably important and that you will forever be. Trauma is not your testimony; overcoming is walking your way to a different ending. Learn not to bypass your triggers; they are the gold, the key to healing your past wounds and hurts. We all lose hope at some point or season in life. Then, we march into a better season. Occasionally, hope finds us. Like a dog following us like a true best friend, a bird singing to us, or someone loving you unconditionally. Hope is a potent influence. It will change your narrative and your mindset. Hope is optimistic. It brings a ray of comfort and sweeps out the gloom. It diminishes fear, and it marinates in reassurance. **Hope IS always here.** HOPE remains present. It has not given up on you. It is steadfast, and it patiently waits until you are ready to embrace it again. Hope changes everything. Never lose hope.

Understand that when you have gained the lesson, you should know which well is poisoning you and run to the cathedrals of life that sprinkle your healing balm. Recognise that the trigger is only the symptom; there is so much more underneath. Most get rid of the trigger only to rinse and repeat the cycle. The solution is to seek the root cause and go to the source. Become an investigator of your triggers and trauma. Refrain from becoming a martyr to your trauma; see it, recognise the pattern, release it, learn, grow, be gentle, know your worth, forgive yourself first, and then forgive others. Your healing is paramount.

Let your story be different from those that were forced to end their lives too soon. The triggered trauma response is not your portion for the conclusion of your life. Keep moving if you feel you are driving through a season of silence. Your identity is your defining characteristic. You do not have to shout it out on command; embrace it and let it nurture life in you, no matter how negative you feel. Never allow your emotions to dictate the path. Let reality be the voice of reason. Look around for evidence and motivating forces around you. If you can find none, remember to say a prayer, and it will be heard.

We have different experiences, and we all need to learn different things, find a glimmer of hope, and nurse it until it reigns. Life is a formidable crux; never let it beat you and give it all you got. Sometimes, people make their problems become yours, which may turn into a negative experience. You may grapple with it but never get stuck in the negative contours of life. Life rarely offers a parallel view, and we learn from every journey, adventure, misfortune, and character. Learn to craft your intuition - discern your internal compass and let it guide you.

Master how to be brave in the face of a storm. Even if you fail, there is always tomorrow for another attempt. Life offers us a nectar-like no other; never reject it. Live, love, laugh, and fight - live even if it just feels like you are existing. Keep on breathing, and the season will most definitely change. How other people behave has nothing to do with you. Do not let the actions of others ruin your inner peace and calm. You control your state of mind and your will to live.

I trekked to South Africa a few months after the funeral, and upon my return, I was no longer the woman I used to be. I gleaned a lot from the trauma, but mostly, I learned who I will never be like. Fragments of me were lost and stripped of dignity. After my return, I began writing this book. It was a birth in the depths of mourning. It is both a tribute to my brother and a glimmer of hope to others who are struggling with suicide, including those who are grappling with the remnants of suicide.

This book will unravel life and journey for you from the pit of despair and showcase the hope that you have in the bleakest season of life. These chapters will bring discernment, knowledge, and tools for you to find your focus and live your best life. God already knows who you are; however, He wants to know who you want to be. Where you are right now does not have to equate to what your future will look like. **"Whosoever shall put their trust in God shall be supported in their trials, their troubles, and their afflictions, and shall be lifted at the last day."– Alma 36:3.** Faith is like Wi-Fi; it is invisible, but it has the power to connect you to what you need. The Word does not say, *"Whosoever shall put their trust in the Lord shall have no trials, troubles, or afflictions."* That is not the promise. We have been sent to earth to be tested, and the test does not disappear when we begin to exercise our faith.

Memories burrowed in me, and sleep eluded me. I had to dig deep to find my balance and shine a light on this taboo topic—suicide. This book is a journey of hope and healing. It explores the sensitive and complex topic of suicide to foster understanding, compassion, and help. This book aims to provide valuable insights, resources, and support to individuals who may be struggling with suicidal thoughts, as well as those who care about them. By addressing the issue openly and honestly, I hope to contribute to the ongoing dialogue surrounding human welfare, look for the signs, and ultimately inspire a positive change in how we approach suicide prevention. It will provide an implementation plan for a safer community. This book is also for you if you lost someone to suicide; it will guide you through the shadows to reach a new, altered equilibrium. My expression confirms that we need to shine a light on human welfare, and my candour will serve up strategic conversations.

I can bear the pain, but not the pain of another human; that is more than I can haul. Out of my own lived experience, I have curated many self-help tools to help you navigate through your journey. These tools will help you feel less adrift and anchor-less in a raging sea. When trauma and grief came pouring over me like water over a broken dam, I felt overwhelmed by the mayhem. These tools will help you navigate and propel you to a better season. The shards of suicide naturally leave us raw, and this book will guide you to a new path. Physical science governs that what goes up must come down. We all have not yet mastered falling so that the injury does not prevent us from rising and trying again. Dig deep and identify conducts that demonstrate inconsistency, then find a remedy to rise just as basic physics demands. This book will help you get up, no matter how many times you have fallen.

It will resonate with your vulnerability and compel you to live your authentic values despite the hurdles. It will showcase the importance of making the wise decision to have those difficult conversations and introspection. If you must squeeze yourself into someone else's mould, then that is the ultimate betrayal. This is an expression to help you break that pattern. When life throws a curveball of despair, chaos, and devastation, it is easy to slip into the shadows of suicide and grief. I yield my duty to share my lived experience with this taboo topic.

This book has a strategized plan for you to find a remedy if you are struggling with suicide or navigating life after you have lost someone to suicide. This book will give you the tools, empathy, and zeal to shift to a new season in life. It will serve your vocation to enhance lives. This book will inspire the reader to rise and do their best in the face of turbulence. As long as you are breathing, everything is achievable. Never quit. Pick up this book and make the rest of your life the best of your life. This book will help you to:

1. Discover all the possibilities despite the limitations
2. Realise the silver lining
3. Sense the palpable and the hidden
4. Achieve the incredible
5. Confirm your destiny, which is unravelled in a season of battle rather than a term of ease
6. The choice to get stronger or linger in agony

It will awaken you from your stupor to watch out for the sacred commotions of your life. These focal moments may seem like turmoil, but they are golden invitations to change this one audacious life radically. As an author, I offer you this opportunity on a platter. I have proposed a charcuterie board of decisions and tools to close the chapter in your life and march on to a better beat.

"Success is not final. Failure is not fatal; it is the courage to continue that counts." - Winston Churchill.

1. Heart to Heart Connection

In 2016, I was engaged in the enjoyable privilege of hosting kin—my brother in Australia. It was the first time in almost 30 years that we were in the same country for a prolonged period. This allowed us to have many heart-to-heart conversations and connections. He opened up to me, and I got a glimpse of his real world.

When he was just nineteen years old, he had an accident at work. He lost the use of his right hand. He was 43 and unlocking the brokenness with me. He was never compensated by the organization for which he was employed. His life took an unexpected detour, and everyone just strapped in and continued the journey. Jayandra could not be commercially employed. He lost the opportunity to be a breadwinner, and with that, he never had the bleakest chance of courtship or matrimony. Yet he still embraced life with the audacity to hope. I could discern the heaviness in his heart when he told me all he wanted were life's simple pleasures. To be married and have his own family. My heart shattered as every potential suitor did not find him suitable due to his disability.

Rejection does not mean you are not good enough; it means that others have overlooked your potential. Seeking validation will keep you trapped; you do not need anyone or anything to prove your worth. Understand this, and you will be free. If external validation is your only source of nourishment, you will be starving for the rest of your life. Always focus on your potential instead of your limitations. Most of us feel fear, and very few act on their hopes. Strength does not come from what you can do but from overcoming what you want to begin.

In developed countries, it is mandatory to undergo work health and safety training. In an unfortunate accident, this is reported, and protocols are followed. Sadly, organisations in developing countries like South Africa may be mandated by legislation, but these protocols are never enforced. The organization he worked for took no responsibility for his welfare, future, or disability. At the tender age of nineteen, he was handed a blow that ended his life metaphorically before it even began. Obstacles do not define you. If you run into a catastrophe, never give up. Find a solution, one step at a time. Conquer one day at a time. Systemic problems are severe and recurrent issues that stem from problems inherent in the design and operation of the disability system. It compounds with funding, policy, cultural, operational, and corruption issues. These systemic problems are interconnected. None of these exist in isolation, and they often have a compounding effect on the quality of life.

Improving the lives of disabled people in South Africa requires a multifaceted approach that addresses the various challenges and barriers they face. Here are some ways that you can make a difference:

Advocate for disability rights: Speak out against discrimination and advocate for policies and laws that protect the rights of disabled people. This can include supporting disability organisations and joining advocacy campaigns.

Promote accessibility: Accessibility is a crucial issue for disabled people, and ensuring that public spaces, transportation, and communication are accessible can make a big difference. You can advocate for accessibility improvements in your community and support businesses and organizations prioritising accessibility.

Support education and employment opportunities: Many disabled people in South Africa face barriers to education and employment, which can limit their opportunities and perpetuate poverty. You can support initiatives that provide education and training opportunities for disabled people and advocate for policies that promote inclusive hiring practices.

Provide support and resources: Disabled people often face additional challenges related to healthcare, transportation, and daily living. You can volunteer with disability organisations or provide support to disabled individuals in your community, such as by offering rides or helping with daily tasks.

Challenge stereotypes and stigma: Disabled people often face negative attitudes and stereotypes that can limit their opportunities and perpetuate discrimination. You can challenge these stereotypes by promoting positive representations of disabled people in the media and your community and by speaking out against ableism.

Improving the lives of disabled people in South Africa requires a sustained effort, and by working together and advocating for change, we can create a more inclusive and equitable society.

An oyster that has not been wounded in any way does not produce pearls. A pearl is a healed wound. Pearls are a product of pain resulting from a foreign or unwanted substance entering the oyster, such as a parasite or a grain of sand. Inside an oyster shell is a shiny substance called "nacre." When a grain of sand enters, the nacre cells go to work and cover the grain of sand with layers and more layers to protect the defenseless body from the oyster. As a result, a beautiful pearl is formed. The more pearls, the more valuable.

God never allows pain without a purpose. What if your most incredible legacy ignites out of your most significant hurt? *__The hard things we may be going through now are really nothing in comparison to the glory that will be revealed in us later. – Romans 8:17-18.__* Jayandra persevered to live an abundant life for 31 years with disability and unemployment.

Living in South Africa with a disability is no walk in the park. There is almost minimal financial support and no tangible support for emotional well-being. To inspire people, do not show them your superpowers, status, or bank balance. Instead, reflect and kindle their strengths. Showcase their abilities, not yours, help them discover, inspire them to develop, mentor them to maximize all their capabilities, show them what they are efficient at, encourage them to grow, and congratulate them on their achievements.

Respect and empathy for someone are about admiring who they are and who they are becoming. Make that choice to appreciate and recognise what God is doing in them. Recognition goes a long way; it is like honour as you give it. You get it. We are all created in the image of God, and thus, we are like precious jewels, but sometimes we forget that others are extraordinary, too. It is your prerogative to revamp the tariff for others to ingress you and brand your self-worth. Never forget that every person has self-worth and value. Know your value, especially when you feel weak. Discern your power even when you find it hard to speak. Identify your authority particularly when others doubt you. Recognise your clout, even when you feel alone. Understand your influence, even when things are falling apart. You will not be intimidated by any circumstances when you understand the power and potential vested in you.

During Jayandra's sojourn to Australia, we created many cherished memories, laughter, and deep conversations. He shared how invisible he felt. I encouraged him to focus on the glass that was half full and not dwell on the empty component. I motivated him to reach for the desires of his heart, and I assured him that I would help him every step of the way. I assured him that the future belongs to those who believe in the beauty of their dreams. Adversity is a given, and courage is a choice. I told him that he always had a choice. I saw his eyes sparkle with hope and new vision. He turned over a new leaf, dreaming of new goals, and I was the wind beneath his wings to encourage and enable him. I recall when he accomplished his first goal - the excitement was surreal. I was thrilled for him, and I was going to deliver in spades.

Jayandra turned the corner and began embracing life and hope; he had a spring in his step. Despite the limitations, he chose his internal guiding force to live his best life. He had finally tapped into the illuminated path beyond the darkness. Your doubts about today will be the only limit to your realisation of tomorrow. Instead of dreading and evading the unknown, acknowledge and embrace it as a birth of possibilities. Your actions will always scream over your emotions. Sometimes, the light that you start to shine will intimidate people, and they will manifest their darkness profoundly. It is easier for them to reject you than to look in the mirror. Our world does not require more successful people. Humanity desperately needs more peacemakers, healers, restorers, storytellers, and those who love unconditionally.

They say it takes a village to raise a child; what about an adult? It takes a village to sustain an adult as well. When Jayandra arrived in Australia, even though South Africa was a by-product of apartheid, the social connotations of Africa did not restrict him. He blended into this cosmopolitan melting pot despite the lack of corporate professional experience. My interstate friend Simon from Queensland visited us in Sydney, and the pair got on like a house on fire. A few weeks later, Simon hopped on another flight to come and spend quality time with Jayandra. And the buck did not stop there. When I visited South Africa, Simon accompanied me to continue his friendship with him. Jayandra did not have social media. He made international friends. It was so authentic that his friend crossed the ocean for him.

Another friend from Sydney, Ross, took to Jayandra like a duck to water. Australian and South African, with no social divides, just genuine camaraderie. Distinctively highlighting the traditional larrikin knack. The pair was so enthused that Jayandra was asked to accompany Ross on his work trips, meeting the Australian clientele at grassroots levels. Jayandra ostentatiously impressed Ross that he asked him to return to Australia and live with him. Despite the cacophony of limitations in his life, some people looked at him and saw a human. When you are not included, invited, or considered, whisper to yourself, "Thank you for the space necessary in my life for the people that matter most to me. I am blessed." Never define your life by the careless ineptitude under the influence of envy that some humans practice. When you look for the good in others, you discover the best in yourself and give others the tenacity to live.

Choose self-esteem, not self-pity. Live by choice and not by chance. Always be motivated and not manipulated. Understand the difference between being helpful and being used. Make the changes, not excuses, and learn to excel, not compete. If I could give my brother anything, I would bless him with an abundance of confidence. So, he would never forget his self-worth, propelling him to chase his dreams and allowing him to discern how I deeply loved him. I tried to push him in tangible ways, but the greed and envy of others in his landscape were too much for him to withstand. People found it unshameful to swindle from a disabled and unemployed person. Fortune and material stuff rarely drop out of the sky and into our lap. It is strategically carved, rarely blessed by a loved one, and sometimes blatantly stolen. The unprincipled rebel cares not how their actions impact other lives. You must endure the rain if you want to enjoy the rainbow. Sometimes, the rain is persistent and unrelenting.

The hope and future I tried to give him were snatched in their infancy. It breaks my heart to write this. Let alone live it. It is the character of very few to honour without envy who has prospered. People need to understand that actions always affect other people. So be careful about what you say and do. It is not always just about you and your agenda. The disrespect is all the closure you need. Some people are jealous because your character carries more weight than the title. They cannot stand to see another human being more blessed than they are. Craft your intuition to be so strong that you not only know who you are but will also discern who others are. Any loss you experience for speaking the truth is not a loss but alignment.

You will not see it for what it is until you stop looking through the lens of what you want it to be. Life itself is a privilege. To live life to the fullest is a choice. Do you talk to your entire life? Clean your body, mind, soul, and spirit, and your house, your car, your network, and your phone. Get everything in alignment. Your energy introduces you before you even speak. Not everyone deserves to have access to your energy. Save your high vibrating energy for those who genuinely care for you. You are a unique soul and made to go the distance. Many wolves will come in sheep clothing. Try to discern who the wolves are in your life and never waste your energy on them, and even if you share DNA with them, purge them. If not, it will cost you dearly. You may even have to pay with your life.

Base your understanding, knowledge, and experience on not stereotyping. Stereotyping reflects your bias. When you treat people fairly, you impose human well-being and respect. Nuances in a person's identity or circumstances should not create disadvantages. Each individual has a rich tapestry and future. Differences and similarities affect behaviour and outcomes for most people; sadly, this should not be the case. There is honour in living in alignment with your morals, values, and ethics. The notion of status and financial accolades creates the illusion that humans are tagged by what they possess or lack. It also gives others the false power to prowl from the disadvantaged. When love and inclusion are limited, it will diminish hope for the most durable person. Suicide is not a mystery; unravel human greed, and you will discover some root cause.

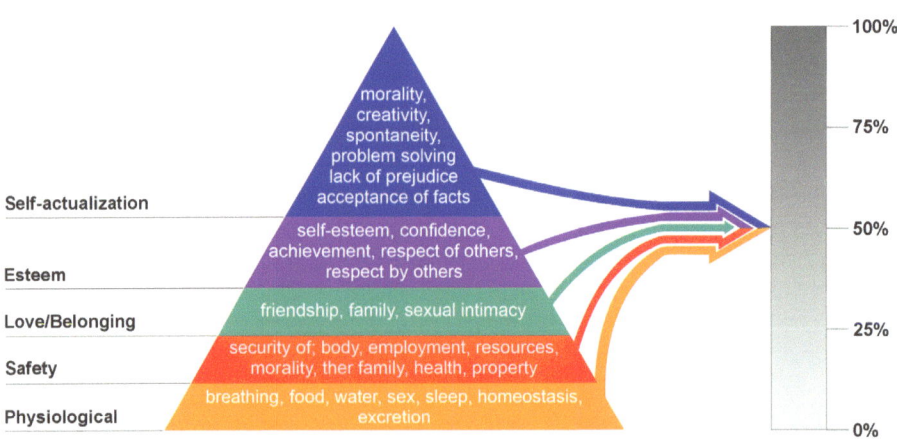

Image 1: A Theory of Human Motivation by Abraham H. Maslow. Adapted to include a scale of satisfaction. On the Right Hand Side how many per cent fulfilment do you have in these aspects of your life?

The theory of human motivation refers to various psychological theories and frameworks that explain why individuals behave the way they do and what drives their actions and goals. One well-known theory in this field is Abraham Maslow's hierarchy of needs.

Abraham Maslow proposed a hierarchical model of human needs in his 1943 paper, "A Theory of Human Motivation." According to Maslow, human needs can be arranged in a pyramid-like structure, with lower-level needs as the foundation for higher-level needs. The hierarchy consists of five levels:

Physiological needs: *These are the most basic survival needs, such as food, water, shelter, sleep, and other bodily requirements.*

Safety needs: *Once physiological needs are met, individuals seek safety and security, including personal and financial security, health, and protection from harm.*

Love and belongingness need: *Once safety needs are fulfilled, individuals desire social connection, love, friendship, and a sense of belonging within family, friendships, and communities.*

Esteem needs: *Once the lower-level needs are satisfied, individuals strive for recognition, achievement, status, respect, and self-esteem.*

Self-actualization needs: *At the top of the hierarchy, self-actualization represents the fulfilment of an individual's highest potential. It involves personal growth, self-discovery, and realizing one's unique talents and abilities.*

According to Maslow, individuals progress through the hierarchy sequentially, with the lower-level needs taking precedence over the higher-level needs. Once a lower-level need is adequately met, it no longer serves as a motivator, and the individual's focus shifts to the next higher-level need.

It is important to note that the theory of human motivation encompasses various theories and models beyond Maslow's hierarchy, including theories of intrinsic and extrinsic motivation, cognitive theories, and social motivation theories. These theories provide additional insights into the complexities of human motivation and the factors that influence behaviour.

On the right-hand side of Figure 1, I have incorporated a scale to measure where you may land with your motivation in your current life. You can use this scale to tackle challenges and change narratives in your life or someone else's life. People are more than the limitations that they endure. Use this to identify the gaps and become proactive in finding a remedy. People do not require your sympathy, but rather that you act and undertake profoundly—help where you can. If concern touches your heart, then never allow it to get misplaced. Complicated is a relative term. It depends on perspective, so grasp this before you refuse to get your hands dirty. An error of judgment is grave and may cost an innocent life. Allow yourself to put your hands on the plough. There is no crisis; the chaos we create and the stories we write become the ships we sail. We all have bounty and wisdom. The ultimate question is how we navigate it.

When inclusions are invited to the party, empathy will be asked to dance. Getting embraced for your difference makes you feel seen, loved, and cared for. Every person wants to be celebrated, regardless of their circumstances. Your value does not decrease based on someone's inability to see your worth or discern what you need. Sometimes, even if people know what you require, they do not care to fill your void. That is a reflection of them. Do not put the keys to your life or happiness in their hands. A self-aware and mature person will have the ability to be authentic, hold robust conversations, and make assessments of these core human needs. The only thing a river knows is to run to the sea. Who does a human run to? Have you created a place to make others feel visible and free to share their heaviness?

With a look that would steal a soul from a man, Whiskey, the dog, had Jayandra eating out of his paw. They were sometimes recalcitrant peers, as Whiskey would follow him out the gate and wonder about Jayandra's adventures. With all the traffic, this was unsafe for Whiskey, so Jayandra had to develop a plan to sneak out. He had to resort to a sojourn to the vegetable garden, placing a ladder against the fence and slinking out without his best friend noticing him. He lavished Whiskey with five-star cuisine and dotted on him. Whiskey would be as mad as a March Hare when he discovered the betrayal, but all was forgiven with a tasty snack. When Jayandra was dead, Whiskey sensed the palatable change. He pushed his way to confirm for himself. His expression was akin to mine—shocked! Whiskey was spinning in the custody of trauma. As I watched the funeral on livestream, Whiskey's loyalty cemented. My heart crinkled yet again as I watched Whiskey push his way to the coffin and kiss Jayandra. Although the man and his best friend will never meet again, they make each other's lives whole.

Dogs have earned the reputation of being men's best friends due to several reasons:

Loyalty: Dogs are known for their unwavering loyalty towards their owners. They form deep emotional bonds with their human companions and are always there to provide companionship, support, and unconditional love. Dogs are known to be highly devoted and will stand by their owners through thick and thin.

Companionship: Dogs are highly social animals and thrive on human interaction. They are eager to be a part of our lives and enjoy spending time with us. Whether going for walks, playing, or simply relaxing together, dogs provide constant companionship and help alleviate loneliness and isolation.

Emotional Support: Dogs have a remarkable ability to sense and respond to human emotions. They can provide comfort and emotional support during times of stress, sadness, or anxiety. Many dogs are trained as therapy or emotional support animals to assist people with various emotional or psychological conditions.

Protection: Dogs have an instinct to protect their territory and loved ones. They serve as excellent watchdogs and can alert their owners to potential dangers or intruders. The presence of a dog in the household can provide a sense of security and peace of mind.

Playfulness and Entertainment: Dogs have a playful and energetic nature that brings joy and entertainment to their owners. They are always up for a game of fetch, a walk in the park, or simply goofing around. Their playful antics and ability to make us laugh help to reduce stress and bring happiness into our lives.

Health Benefits: Owning a dog has been associated with various health benefits. Regular exercise, like walking or playing with a dog, can improve physical fitness and overall well-being. Dogs have also been shown to positively impact mental health, reducing stress, anxiety, and depression.

Overall, the deep bond, unwavering loyalty, companionship, emotional support, protection, and joy that dogs bring into our lives make them widely regarded as man's best friend—such profound attributes from an animal. Sometimes, you reach a natural inflection point with humans living a quid pro quo lifestyle. Take comfort knowing you can adapt in stewardship, style, and approach with unconditional devotion and sincere loyalty to a pet. Your sense of duty is to find your responsibility in this landscape. If humans have let you down, find comfort in other wholesome avenues. As Jesus said: ***"The wheat and the weeds grow together until the time of harvest." -* Matthew 13:24-30.** Only you can decide what you prefer to invest in and eventually harvest in life! When you make someone else responsible for your despair, you also make them accountable for your joy. Never give anyone that power.

"She was so powerful, not because she was not scared but because she went on so strongly, despite the fear." - Atticus.

2. Unravelling the Complexity

One of the hardest decisions to make in life is to choose which bridge to burn and which bridge to cross. Being loved is the minimum. Ensure you are respected, prioritised, supported, heard, and understood. You can spend more time trying to teach others your song, or you can go where the music is already playing. Find your people. Loving you is easy for those who are in harmony. Consistency is more challenging when no one is clapping for you. It would help to have the courage to clap for yourself during those times. It would be best if you always were your biggest fan. Your anointed oil cost you years, tears, scars, pain, and obedience. Never let anyone play with it. Always remember that what you do in the dark puts you in the light. Always pay attention to those who talk but do not act, those who promise but never deliver, and those who offer lip service but certainly not action.

Thrust by a degree of distressing distraction: the plunge in temperature coupled with the waning sun. To make matters worse, it begins to rain with an unexpected ferocity. This forecast can make anyone's life look bleak. Jayandra was disabled and unemployed, but Mark saw the blessings lavished on him. He decided to lace his agenda with honey and ask Jayandra to help him fix his business vehicle by coercing a cash handout. With nothing but a heart of gold, Jayandra chose to share what was given to him and handed cash to him. Mark took from the disabled and then swindled the rest. My brother was in tears when he narrated this to me. After Jayandra was dead, Mark dared to say that Jayandra had sent him a message with a picture of a noose a year ago, saying, "You are pushing me to suicide." I was mortified when I discovered this and asked Mark what he did with this critical data. Mark responded by pointing the finger. This left the devastation of pondering if this gross ordeal could have been prevented. Always remember that the people who try to drag you down are often the ones who do not have wings that could ever match your height.

Be careful who you trust and help. Some will survive because of your help, and they will have no shame in killing you in the process. You will end up disappointed if you think people will do as much for you as you do for them. Not everyone has the same heart as you.

Be selective about who you help.

Image 2: The reality of trusting people with the wrong agenda.

A phenomenal bird is known as a "fire hawk" or "fire kite." Behaviour observed in certain raptor species, including the Black Kite, in Australia. Fire kites deliberately pick up burning twigs or sticks from active wildfires and carry them to unburnt areas nearby. Dropping these fire-carrying materials ignites new fires, which flush out prey like insects, rodents, or small reptiles. This conduct provides the kites with easier access to food sources trying to escape the spreading fire. This fascinating behaviour has been documented in various parts of Australia, particularly during the dry season when wildfires are more prevalent. It showcases these birds' adaptive nature and ability to exploit fire as a foraging strategy. However, it is important to note that not all kites engage in this behaviour, and it is not unique to Australia; similar observations have also been reported in other parts of the world.

Researchers have studied this behaviour to better understand its ecological significance and impact on fire spread. It provides insights into various ecosystems' complex interactions between wildlife and fire. It is fascinating how humans have adapted to find easy prey rather than work hard for their profits. Unethical characters are always competing for spoils. Unfortunately, innocent people get trapped in their equations. When someone goes the extra mile for a feed, regardless of who they hurt, you get to see exactly who they are, which is ugly. Never try to shine a light on darkness so evil as to ever make a spark. Do not try to understand. Walk over the stones that have been thrown and move to a brighter place. In this life, you will be called to be a protector, provider, lover, and fighter, and the most valuable you will ever add is when you are always the survivor.

> **Never be a character that creates a fire to feed yourself, innocent lives are lost in the pursuit.**

Image 3: A fire hawk starts a fire on purpose.

Furthermore, Mark's family swindled more money by purchasing two other vehicles. The fact that Jayandra was disabled and unemployed did not stop their treacherous conduct. Then more money was extorted for mechanical repairs without proof of what was repaired, yet the vehicle still malfunctioned in all its basic functionalities. Repeated requests were made for transactions that should have legally been provided at the onset. But it was in vain. It was in vain that the culprits tried every trick in the book to be evasive and then hide behind other spineless characters. It made the unfortunate death of Jayandra appear meaningless, as the wicked did not learn a lesson. The perverse force prevailed and then recruited more members to their army - disgusting morals indeed. When you ask people to help and you carry the bricks, they are not the ones to build with. Be gentle when someone reveals their scars to you. It takes more courage to remove one's armour than to assemble it.

Recognising the importance of early intervention in suicide is crucial for addressing this serious human welfare issue. Early intervention refers to identifying and providing support to individuals who may be at risk of suicide before they reach a crisis point. Here are some key reasons why early intervention is significant in preventing suicide:

Increased chances of successful intervention: When warning signs and risk factors are identified early, there is a greater opportunity to intervene effectively and prevent a suicide attempt. Early recognition allows for timely access to appropriate mental health services and support.

Addressing underlying issues: Many individuals who contemplate suicide often experience mental health challenges such as depression, anxiety, or abuse. Early intervention enables professionals to assess and address these underlying issues, providing appropriate treatment and support before they worsen.

Reduction of stigma: Early intervention efforts help reduce the stigma of seeking help. By promoting open conversations and providing support at an early stage, individuals are more likely to feel comfortable discussing their concerns and seeking assistance without fear of judgement.

Building coping skills: Early intervention allows individuals to learn and develop effective coping strategies to manage stress, emotions, and challenging situations. By equipping people with the necessary skills and resources early on, they can better navigate life's difficulties and reduce the risk of suicidal thoughts and behaviours.

Creating a support network: Early intervention involves engaging the individual's support network, including friends, family, and professionals. By involving trusted individuals in the process, there is an increased likelihood of identifying warning signs, providing appropriate support, and reducing isolation.

Prevention through education: Early intervention efforts often focus on raising awareness about suicide risk factors, warning signs, and available resources. Educating the public, including schools, communities, and workplaces, helps increase recognition of suicidal ideation and encourages prompt action to prevent self-harm.

Saving lives: Ultimately, early intervention saves lives. By recognising the importance of early intervention and implementing effective strategies, we can provide the necessary support to individuals at risk of suicide, preventing tragic outcomes and promoting human well-being.

It is important to remember that early intervention should be part of a comprehensive approach to suicide prevention, which includes destigmatizing mental health, promoting access to mental health services, and fostering supportive communities. Removing toxic people from the landscape is difficult, and those who exhibit "fire kite" bird behaviour ought to be addressed professionally with legal constraints.

Suicide is a complex and multifaceted issue that involves various psychological, social, and environmental factors. It is important to approach the topic with sensitivity and understanding. Despite all the conventional signs to look out for, sometimes the well that we are drinking from is poisoned, and we have no hope at all. Be cautious about who you build your life with. Not everyone in your circle has your best interests at heart. Emotional intelligence is the most significant factor to consider when you prioritise your welfare. Life is about writing and rewriting; if you do not like what is on the page, rewrite it. There are plenty of blank pages. Other factors to consider when prioritising your welfare:

Mental health factors: Mental health plays a significant role in suicide risk. Conditions such as depression, anxiety disorders, bipolar disorder, schizophrenia, and substance abuse disorders can increase the likelihood of suicidal thoughts or actions. These conditions often involve biological, psychological, and environmental factors.

Social factors: Social factors can contribute to suicidal ideation. Feelings of loneliness, social isolation, lack of social support, or being exposed to bullying, harassment, or discrimination can all impact an individual's mental well-being. Relationship problems, such as the loss of a loved one, a breakup, or family conflicts, can also increase suicide risk.

Environmental factors: Environmental factors can have a significant influence on suicide rates. Access to lethal means, such as firearms or toxic substances, can increase the risk. Additionally, exposure to suicide within one's family, peer group, or community can contribute to a contagion effect known as "suicide clustering."

Cultural factors: Cultural attitudes and beliefs around suicide can vary greatly, affecting help-seeking behaviours and the overall stigma associated with mental health issues. Some cultures may have stronger taboos surrounding suicide, making it difficult for individuals to discuss their struggles or seek support openly.

Protective factors: It is vital to acknowledge protective factors that can help reduce the risk of suicide. These factors include strong social support networks, access to mental health resources and treatment, effective coping skills, positive problem-solving abilities, and a sense of purpose or meaning in life.

Prevention and support: Suicide prevention efforts involve various strategies, including increasing awareness, promoting mental health literacy, reducing stigma, and providing accessible and affordable mental health services. Crisis hotlines, support groups, therapy, and counselling are some of the resources available for those in need. Encouraging open and non-judgmental conversations about mental health can also help create a supportive environment.

Remember, while discussing suicide in an educational context, it is crucial to approach the topic with empathy, respect, and caution. If you or someone you know is struggling with suicidal thoughts, reach out to a mental health professional or a helpline in your country for immediate assistance.

We have a plethora of insights on how to manage personal productivity. We are bombarded with the fundamentals of organising obligations, ambitions, and habits to competently and dependably complete what matters most. What is most important to you strikes a chord with me. Time, energy, resources, outcome, and ethics contribute to the equation. No matter how intelligently intentional you are about your productivity and integrity, it will form a base of brouhaha if it is conceited and shallow. You may have ticked off the stereotype checkboxes. "It's the value of the deeds you get done." Can you sense the advantage of your existence to tick off boxes? Come to the corporate round table and the circle of life to find versions of your humble self and birth authentic productivity and a lifestyle that oozes integrity.

In January 2021, the world woke up to the news that New Zealand's Prime Minister, Jacinda Arden, genuinely reflected on her productivity and decided to resign. *"I no longer have enough in the tank to do it justice."* These were the words from Jacinda Ardern, New Zealand's youngest Prime Minister in 150 years, announcing her decision to step down from the role on February 7, 2021. *"I'm a politician who is first and foremost a human,"* Ardern said of the announcement, explaining that after six *"challenging"* years, she felt she would be doing a *"disservice to New Zealand"* if she continued in the job. In 2019, Ardern spoke with LinkedIn News. Here are some key takeaways:

On balance: *"Pick something important to you and be disciplined about that one thing."*

On allyship in politics: *"The idea of supportive environments and politics doesn't always seem like they go together. In every workplace, we should be trying to create environments where we do look out for one another."*

Advice for women entering the workforce: *"There are lots of times when things will get tough. Always back yourself."*

On flexibility in the workplace: *"We're not beings who exist over here in compartments at work and over here in life… We need to keep making sure we are creating environments where people can juggle those responsibilities."*

How important is it for **YOU** to speak up about your well-being, the welfare of others, and where humanity is heading? How do you assess what you have *'in the tank?'* What changes will you make to your productivity and integrity? Are you content with the status quo of just ticking the boxes and remaining on your path? What is a human-first approach to you? What insights are you leaving the world with while you are productive and upright? You need to chew on your contemplating pen and establish what your tentative outline is and what partially hems you in. We have stubborn populism and carnal incontinence regarding the truth about productivity and honesty. We all boast the status of being busy and achieving. What are we accomplishing? Does your ethics shrink the platform of meaningful ascent? This self-examination may be gleefully brutalising, but you must enhance your objectives and life.

Step away from just ticking boxes and regard yourself as moral and innovative. Escape appropriately contrite with new zeal to focus on what makes our world, community, family, and life better. Put your hand at the helm and make it matter with the time, effort, and resources you use. Become acutely aware of how **YOUR YIELD** can change the narrative. There exists a form of asymmetry with obliging approaches and proposals. Understanding that lives are derailed and many still live in a bubble due to a noteworthy intellectual and cultural gap. Compassion for all discrimination and corruption experienced globally requires acknowledgment and rectification to save lives. Zooming into the extensive posture of the spectrum from responsibilities to scrutiny. Mandating the process to include, but not be limited to, this scheme of targeted solutions can form the justification for change:

Prowling the disadvantaged: Your real ethics are highlighted

Creating better mental health outcomes: Be proactive to establish healthier people

Organizations that shy away from legal obligations: How do you bridge this gap?

Impartial collaboration: How productive are you about this?

A plan to decline the systemic discrimination culture: What creativity have you sparked with this?

Rational destabilisation of inhumane laws: Output is the real intelligence.

Conviction of acts of cruelty: Efficiency tells the story

Conscious awareness of negative culture and behaviour: Yields with action

Insight to bias: The ostrich syndrome is not productive

Custodianship clause: What part do you play in the equation?

Decolonisation legislature: How do you close the gap regarding psychological aspects of the colonial experience?

Authentic liberation: Where do you stand?

Call out and address community, society, national, and international rhetoric: How are you doing that now?

The practice of genuine UBANTU: Act like you mean it

Create a global Royal Commission Standard of guiding principles: Vital productivity

Regardless of citizenship, culture, or creed, every race should be factored into the ethics of a solution. An execution that spawns and generates variable manifestations of healing. Change the narrative from complacency to fresh accountability. Create global industry standards for recognised practices, enforce Royal Commission standards, and introduce hefty penalties when actions are not challenged or changed after the problems are identified. Refrain from just ticking boxes; comprehend, model, and action PRODUCTIVITY AND INTEGRITY IN YOUR SOLUTIONS. Truth is hyped. What makes a material difference is the quality that you produce. Was the effort valuable? "Intelligence without ambition is a bird without wings." - Salvador Dali. Productivity is not just using your time, money, and energy wisely. It makes a difference in what you produce, inspire, and kill.

What is authentic productivity to you? Plausibly persistent with your progressive patronage, assets aplenty, leader of the pack, flock tactics, still grappling with the sins of the past and the struggle to atone, honing in the vicissitudes of management styles, sitting in opulent silence, reunited with the surrendered mobile phone, or simply illustrating portraits of academic poise with hints of esteem. We are all fashioned differently; dabble in seeking what gives vital productivity meaning to you, then live by it. Breathe it, permit it to fashion you and the world in prominent ways. ***"Whatever you do, do well. For when you go to the grave, there will be no work or planning or knowledge or wisdom." -* Ecclesiastes 9:10.** This scripture offers insight into living an uncut life.

Substantiate your life with meaningful pursuits. Keep yourself busy with activity - action that makes a material difference. Take accountability for what is entrusted to you as a custodian. Why bother to do anything in an average way? If it is worth doing, then do it with excellence. Never get trapped in a culture of entitlement, demanding a reward to match your effort. Reward yourself by living according to your highest values. You cannot be productive at anything when you are not equipped with the right tools. Mindset, ambition, knowledge, honesty, and wisdom are the greatest tools. Exhibit multilateral dignity towards yourself and others, and never bite the hands that feed you. When lies connect people, the truth will eventually separate them - tragically, sometimes it is even death.

As a prodigal returning to South Africa, one of my frequent favourites was to permeate myself with local connections. On this trip, I saw the real calibre of hearts that pretended to love my brother. Haunts as a sibling continue to date. Suicide is a complicated experience, and support is the basic mantra to navigate this terrain. Unfortunately, the *"fire hawk"* bird behaviour sometimes persists even after a loved one has passed on. When souls are mourning, one would naturally assume that contriving will seize. Pay attention to those that belong to the *"fire hawk"* nest. Protect your welfare and obtain legal representation if you need to. Open yourself up to show others who you are with your told and untold stories, even when they model a flagrant disregard for human welfare. Life is forever altered, and Jayandra will not breathe again to save any broken heart. With the progression of time, he found it easier to die than to continue with the circle of life - a dense grey intrusion of melancholy stoops down some of those left behind. Never permit the "fire hawk" characters to claim another life.

1. Most suicidal thinkers have no intention of dying. They prefer for their emotions or circumstances to change.

2. With or without intervention, all our emotions eventually change, and thus circumstances, so it is possible to ignore your feelings and wait for a better season. Never find a permanent solution to a temporary problem.

3. Most suicidal thinkers sentimentalize their deaths by suicide by never considering the reality of a failed attempt and the damage it does both emotionally and physically.

4. Suicidal thinkers may deem this the best revenge. However, cutting out your nose to spite your face is no revenge.

"The secret, Alice, is to surround yourself with people who make your heart smile. It is then, only then, that you will find wonderland." - Lewis Carroll.

3. Human Welfare

The world will ask you who you are, and if you do not know, the world will tell you. I watched an Australian documentary that made me marvel at the similarities between the animal and human kingdoms. A dingo pup was struggling in a dam of water. The younger one was still wet behind the ears and was stressed in vain trying to climb up a steep bank. Meanwhile, an adult dingo perched on the hill above watched the tragedy unfold; she made no effort to assist and did not flinch a muscle. Eventually, the pup stops trying to get out from sheer exhaustion. Suddenly, a sibling comes at lightning speed from the bush and guides the exhausted dingo to a shallow point, eventually to safety. In the pandemonium of life, some characters will reveal who they are when you need them the most, leaving all their elegance behind them. When you discover a person's character, allow the pain to find a purpose. Understand what you are fighting to achieve rather than contemplating destroying it.

Mark's daughter, Maxine, refused to furnish Jayandra with sales transactions to confirm how his money was spent. He asked for what he was legally entitled to for over a year, and eventually, he was riddled with trauma. After his death, they still refused to furnish the paperwork. Maxine then dared to say, *"This is not his first suicide attempt."* Manifestation began when I inquired about what she did with this fundamental information that could have potentially saved his life. Trust is earned when action meets words. Concern yourself about the blood that you cannot wash off. What remains is the testimony of your character: malicious intentions, contrived outcomes, and manipulation. Who are you, the adult dingo that sits and watches the demise or the sibling dingo that raced to the rescue? ***"Someone will be attracted to your light; others will fear it." Decide to shine anyway." - unknown.*** Mark and Maxine chose not to introspect after an innocent person lost his life. Scene two of the malicious act unfolded. They recruited Jayandra's legal representation to indulge in malpractice rather than serve justice willingly. Welcome to professional characters who create their law even when a life is lost. Anything rolls in for the sake of ego, pride, and tracheary.

Real professional advantage does not come from status or qualification. It comes from the content of your heart. Some will climb over you to get to the top without a second thought. Always remember that money may pay the bills but can never warm a cold heart. Some people will never grow. They never learn their lesson. They will never recognise their mistakes, they will never acknowledge their falls, and they will never admit they were wrong. You will never receive an apology from them, and sadly, you will never see their behaviour change. So, never make it your life's pursuit to change a character without a desire to change. Walk away with your peace intact. When you lose people who treat you poorly, it is not a loss; you are gaining. You exist in co-existence, but you thrive in freedom, where you are valued and treated appropriately with respect. Lifelong learning is only part of the equation. The critical aspect of complimenting a lifelong journey is the lifelong application of the hard lessons. **"Keep your heels, head, and standards high." - Coco Chanel.**

The truth is not for sale, and it never will be. Even the dead speak so clearly if only you care to listen. Humanity must preserve the character of the deceased, regardless of how the guilty parties threaten. Maxine then began creating gossip about Jayandra's character and the legacy of a pure sibling connection. Repainting him with her brush will change the 50 years of authentic history that we shared. Despite international borders, Jayandra and I spoke regularly, and we knew what made each other tick and precisely what was heavy on each heart. Watching Maxine come up with her narrative just cemented her unethical character - anything to push people to suicide and then dig a bigger hole to bury them. Do not let the ugly in others kill the beauty in you. The search for wisdom is perverted by the desire for wealth, status, and social swank - some will even kill for it. Human welfare - what concept is that? We live in a harsh world that does not have the self-awareness to identify and manage human welfare.

The hardest pill you will ever have to swallow is realising that you meant nothing to people that meant so much to you. Never allow loyalty to keep you in situations from which common sense should have liberated you. Karma knows every address and will chase down every person who broke you when you had nothing but good intentions. When someone helps you when they are struggling too, that does not help; that is seva[1], a selfless service. Some have eyes and hearts purely for decorative purposes. The absence of compassion and empathy is disquieting. To the oppressed and trodden, death smells like musk. I watched my kin treated with treachery before and after his death. Time does nothing to dull the sharpness of some tongues. Never assume the price of compassion is too high; wait until you get the bill for regret. Even if the peas are falling off your plate, refuse to lose your integrity and destroy a person's soul. Always aim to bring honour and peace into their obit even when it costs you a high price. The Bible models this to us in this scripture: **Mark 10:41-45, "Even Jesus did not come to be served, but to serve and to give His life as a ransom for many."**

Until you make the unconscious conscious, it will direct your life, and you will call it fate. You are not what happened to you; you are most definitely who you choose to become.

In the skies above, an eagle spotted a sinuous serpent weaving through the tall grass below. With keen eyesight and lightning-fast reflexes, the majestic

---

1   Seva is a Hindi word - the English translation is a service

bird of prey angled its wings and dove swiftly towards its unsuspecting target. Sensing the shadow cast by the eagle's presence, the snake raised its head, flicking its tongue in alarm. But it was too late - the eagle was already upon it. The bird extended its powerful talons, their sharp claws poised for the strike. With a sudden lunge, the eagle snatched the snake in its grasp, the force of its grip constricting the serpent's body. The snake, writhing and coiling, attempted to free itself from the eagle's clutches, its venomous fangs striking out in a desperate defence.

Undeterred, the eagle maintained its grip and began ascending into the sky again, carrying its captive with it. The snake thrashed and wriggled, its body twisting and turning to break free, but the eagle's hold remained unyielding.

As they ascended higher into the heavens, the eagle's aerial prowess became evident. It skilfully maneuvers through the currents, its mighty wings providing stability and control. On the other hand, the snake was at a disadvantage; its elongated body was struggling to maintain balance amidst the wind and the eagle's firm grip. It is unaccustomed to the air and this unnatural environment. With each passing moment, the snake's struggles weakened. The high altitude, combined with the relentless grasp of the eagle, took its toll. The serpent's movements grew sluggish, and its attempts to strike at its captor became feeble.

Satisfied with its conquest, the eagle reached a point where it could go no higher. With a final show of dominance, it released its hold on the exhausted snake, letting it plummet towards the earth below. As the snake descended, it spiralled downward, resembling a graceful dance of defeat. Dazed and disoriented from its mid-air ordeal, it landed with a soft thud. The eagle circled overhead, a triumphant silhouette against the sky, before soaring off into the distance, its hunt successfully concluded.

The encounter ended with the eagle's victory. It serves as a reminder of the constant struggle for survival in the natural world - a relentless cycle where the predator and prey engage in aerial battles, each employing their unique strengths and adaptations to ensure survival. The operative word is "survival." In life, some humans gradually regain their strength while others never recover. People may try to spread their wings once more and soar, forever marked by the encounter with the venomous snake. A testament to the untamed and unpredictable nature of the natural world may be too much for a person to endure. Sometimes, people never comprehend that they burn bridges with people still on them. A person's character is not defined by how they handle victory but by how one swims through the muddy waters of defeat. If you are going to survive, you must love life more than sharks love blood. Spend your day being useful despite your emotions.

How does a broken person bear the weakness of others? Your silence does not bode well for ignoring human injustices. My unconditional heart calls your name constantly, Jayandra. As winter turns to spring, the tune of the wind welcomes nature's splendour, and Mother Nature shares her secrets of a fruitful bounty. How often do you help humans change the seasons in their lives? Never be long on rhetoric and short on specific action; it may cost a life. Not everyone is strong enough to hold on, brave enough to say goodbye to toxic people, and resilient enough to do both without hesitation. Our loved ones must be protected from low-vibrating, inauthentic, and non-reciprocating characters. Your soul is attracted to people like flowers are attracted to the sun. Surround yourself with only those who want to see you grow.

What a serendipitous surprise! Tomorrow may prove less important than yesterday. Let life teach you to cherish the now. The truth carries a way that no lie can be counterfeited, so become a person who creates awareness and reduces barriers that kill people. It is not the stab in the back that kills you. When you turn around and see who is holding the knife, this reality will leave you grappling. How do you nurture healthy relationships and practice compassion? Do you build a supportive society? How have you encouraged open conversations, and when? You do not need to be saved. You need to be heard, seen, and appreciated for who you are. Nurturing resilience in individuals prone to suicidal thoughts is an important and sensitive matter. Here are some strategies that can help:

Promote open communication: Encourage individuals to express their feelings and thoughts in a safe and non-judgmental environment. Let them know it is okay to talk about their struggles and that you are there to listen. If you open up to toxic people who will not champion your welfare, then do not give up. Find people who care.

Foster a support network: Help individuals build a strong support system of trusted friends, family members, or support groups. Having people who can provide emotional support and understanding can significantly impact their resilience.

Encourage professional help: Encourage individuals to seek professional help from mental health practitioners such as therapists, counsellors, or psychiatrists. These professionals can provide therapy, medication, and specialised guidance tailored to the individual's needs.

Provide education: Educate individuals about mental health, suicidal ideation, and risk factors. They can better recognise warning signs and seek help by increasing their knowledge and understanding.

Teach coping skills: Help individuals develop effective coping mechanisms and strategies to manage stress, anxiety, and negative emotions. This may include techniques such as mindfulness, deep breathing exercises, journaling, or engaging in hobbies they enjoy.

Promote self-care: Encourage individuals to prioritise self-care activities that promote physical, emotional, and mental well-being. This can include getting regular exercise, eating a balanced diet, maintaining a consistent sleep schedule, and engaging in activities they find pleasurable and fulfilling.

Focus on strengths and achievements: Help individuals identify and acknowledge their strengths. This can boost their self-esteem and provide a sense of purpose, contributing to their resilience.

Encourage problem-solving: Teach individuals problem-solving skills to help them navigate difficult situations and challenges. Assist them in breaking down problems into manageable steps and finding constructive solutions.

Create a safety plan: Collaborate with the individual to develop a safety plan that outlines steps they can take when experiencing suicidal thoughts or in crisis. This plan may involve reaching out to trusted individuals, using helplines, or seeking immediate professional assistance.

Follow-up and check-in: Regularly check the individual's well-being and provide ongoing support. Let them know that you are there for them and that they are not alone in their journey towards resilience.

Remember, it is crucial to involve mental health professionals when working with individuals prone to suicidal thoughts. As you feel yourself separating from survival mode, you will glean what the other aromas of life have to offer. Eventually, you will experience what it feels like to be safe. This is what wholesome love is. If someone is in immediate danger or at risk of harming themselves, contact emergency services in your country right away.

Logotherapy is a psychotherapeutic approach developed by Viktor Frankl, an Austrian psychiatrist and Holocaust survivor. It is based on the belief that humans are motivated by a sense of purpose and meaning in life. Logotherapy derives its name from the Greek word "logos," meaning "meaning." According to logotherapy, the primary motivation for human beings is the search for meaning. Frankl believed that individuals could find meaning and purpose even in the most challenging and painful circumstances. He emphasised the importance of personal responsibility and the freedom to choose one's attitude in any given situation, regardless of the external circumstances.

Logotherapy focuses on helping individuals identify and pursue their unique sense of meaning and purpose. It aims to assist individuals in becoming aware of the values and beliefs that guide their lives and to encourage them to engage in activities and relationships that align with their sense of meaning. By helping individuals find meaning, logotherapy alleviates psychological distress, existential emptiness, and a sense of meaninglessness. One of the key techniques used in logotherapy is *"de-reflexion,"* which involves shifting the individual's focus away from their problems and towards meaningful goals and the well-being of others. Frankl believed that individuals could find purpose and meaning in life by transcending oneself, contributing to the well-being of others, or dedicating oneself to a cause greater than oneself. Logotherapy is a humanistic and existential approach to psychotherapy that focuses on the search for meaning and purpose as a central aspect of human existence. It aims to help individuals overcome psychological challenges by facilitating the discovery and pursuit of their unique sense of meaning.

All humans must endure varying levels of difficult situations in their lives. When you cannot change the situation, the only thing you can do is change your attitude towards it. Think of a current or recent situation that is troubling you, and answer the questions accordingly:

Analysis Prompts	Personal Response
Describe the event	
How has this event impacted you negatively?	
How has this event impacted you positively?	
How would you look at the situation differently?	
Pause and think about the bigger picture. What purpose does this event serve in your life?	
How can you benefit from this event?	
What lessons have you learned from this event?	

Be the person who still tries after failure, following frustration and exhaustion, even with heartache and deception. Then, may the quality of the people you attract reflect the healing and hard work you have put into creating a new version of yourself. When you begin to wonder whether you can trust someone or not, that is when the red flags should be flying high. It is okay if you do not have everything figured out; you do not have to. However, give it all you have every day as you prepare for the next day. Reach a place where you prioritise and make deliberate choices to protect your mental, emotional, and spiritual welfare.

When life becomes overwhelming, taking a step back and prioritising self-care is essential. First and foremost, acknowledging your feelings and seeking support from friends, family, or a therapist is crucial. Take time to assess your commitments and responsibilities and be willing to say no to additional tasks if necessary. Incorporating stress-relief practices into your daily routine, such as mindfulness, meditation, or exercise, can help you manage stress. Break down tasks into smaller, manageable steps to make them less daunting. Remember to set aside time for activities that bring you joy and relaxation. Ultimately, finding a balance between self-care, seeking support, and managing responsibilities is key to navigating overwhelming periods in life. Taking offence is a choice; you are defeated when you allow someone's opinion to define you.

A professional colleague with whom I am acquainted is a successful business owner. He was on an international trip and, unfortunately, had a health scare due to an adverse reaction to food poisoning. Upon his return to Australia, he had to undergo major surgery and post-operation, he found himself in a dark place. He was overwhelmed with life, and when sleep eluded him, he decided to swim and not sink any more. He self-introspected and wrote this in his journal to keep himself afloat. He eventually made it safely to the brighter side. Even the strongest and the most positive can find themselves helpless at times. Cues drive the mind. The strongest are emotions.

Defining helplessness

Typically, this is the feeling of being unable to control your situation, environment, or outcome. Recovering from an illness is a great example. One is at the mercy of time. It takes time to heal; it is not in your control. During recovery, emotions are driven by one's analysis of one's current situation. Surgery may slow you down; your pace is slow, and you realise it takes you longer to get to where you want to go.

You may not be able to lift things. Others are mindful and helpful, but this then makes one realise that they are not as strong as they used to be. The mind converts this emotion to a feeling of weakness. The general posture is also affected. One can easily succumb to this spiral of negative feelings, and confidence is impacted.

Problem-solving abilities are affected

The mood, the emotional state at a particular moment, determines your ability to react to issues and problems. It is inevitable that during illness and recovery, confidence is deflated. One's approach to problems is different in this state.

Issues seem more intense than when your mood is more positive. One also tends to compound the problems and have the feeling of not being able to address them.

Helplessness can creep in.

How to deal with this - My happy place

Everyone is different, and it is all about controlling your emotions. I tend to take myself to what I call the valley of happiness. This "valley" is a collection of happy memories. It could include places I visited with someone dear, family moments, a hug from someone I cherish, etc. This is probably one of the few benefits of dwelling on the past.

I then delve deeper and try to multiply those memories. This has a profound effect on my mood and emotions.

Frameworks for problem-solving are essential

Once I have controlled my emotions, I apply the framework I usually use. I tend to fall back on the **SQuARE** method.

1. Analyse the situation
2. What is the key question or issue?
3. What are possible alternatives and answers?
4. Choose the recommendation
5. Evaluate the solution.

Good night!

Healing requires hard conversations. In addition, your healing requires soft exchanges. You can alter your emotions and never become a slave to what they present to you each time. You can adopt the A, B, and C techniques:

A = Anchor yourself in facts, not fluctuating emotions.

B = Behaviour patterns should be analysed and identify ways to improve.

C = Celebrate your small and big wins

When the negative voices from others pierce your mind, pray that your spirit will filter out all the noise. Understand what it is to live on the edge of a new normal and equip yourself with the tools to succeed. Excerpt from my co-authored book *Heart Warrior*: "I discovered first-hand that regardless of my intentions, dogma, constructive innovation or attitude, if an organization or people are devoted to misinterpreting you, they already have drawn a conclusion void of facts. They will resort to manipulating the details. There is always a victim and a perpetrator. Make a reconciliation with which end of the spectrum you are in. Find your poise no matter how devastating reality is. I dwelled with certain storms. I gleaned to exist with fragments of splendour in a mountain of agony – complete in my corporate attire, delivering my deliverables professionally. The warrior's heart was always there, yet no one cared to take a peek." I can make the keyboard hum, but the real victory is when you live this.

"Sometimes we are just collateral damage in someone else's war against themselves." - Lauren Eden.

4. Listening to the Silent Cry

The real voyage of discovery consists not of seeking new landscapes but of having a new vision. I am still reconciling my trudge through life without my brother. His shrieking loud cries for help were ignored and disregarded. How you treat others is a unique voice and a telling tale of the truth about what matters to you and precisely what you feel about the person crying for help. God does not make furniture; He created the trees and inspired humans to be creative. How do you excel with your creativity when it comes to humans? Our landscape offers so many inspiring stories to develop our character and values. I watched a farmer in Australia rise to the occasion with his creativity to help Koalas by building water troughs during droughts.

Koalas in Australia face numerous challenges, including habitat loss, climate change, and drought. While water scarcity during droughts can harm koala populations, the primary threat to their survival is not the lack of water but rather the loss of suitable habitat and food sources. Koalas are highly specialised marsupials that rely primarily on eucalyptus leaves as their primary source of nutrition. Eucalyptus trees have evolved to be highly efficient at extracting and conserving water, meaning the leaves they produce have a low water content. Consequently, koalas have adapted to obtain their hydration needs mainly from the moisture in the eucalyptus leaves they consume rather than from external water sources.

During drought, eucalyptus trees may produce leaves that contain even less water, which can challenge koalas to meet their hydration requirements. However, the primary concern for koalas during a drought is the loss of suitable eucalyptus trees and the decline in the quality and quantity of the available leaves. Droughts can lead to decreased eucalyptus leaf production and increased leaf toxins, making them less nutritious and potentially harmful to koalas. Additionally, habitat loss due to human activities such as land clearing, urbanisation, and deforestation is a significant threat to koalas. When their habitat is destroyed, koalas are forced to move into fragmented areas with limited food resources, increasing their vulnerability to drought and other stressors.

Conservation efforts are crucial to protecting koalas and their habitats. These include initiatives such as habitat restoration, reforestation, wildlife corridors, and the establishment of protected areas. Furthermore, managing land use practices, reducing greenhouse gas emissions, and addressing climate change are necessary steps to mitigate the impacts of drought and preserve suitable habitats for koalas and other wildlife in Australia.

We have undoubtedly found ways to be creative in helping the koalas. I cannot help but look at the parables of human plight. Who looks out for a human's natural habitat if the source of nutrition becomes toxic? When Jayandra was blessed with the resources to purchase a vehicle, he reached out to his tribe, both family and friends. Most were too envious to stop and help him accomplish this basic dream. He toiled for 31 years as a disabled, unemployed man, and that was the vision box that people wanted him to remain in. They were not evolved enough to lift a finger, show unconditional love, or grow some empathy. Life is a way to share the truth. They all shared their truth with him, and yes, it certainly did speak to him loud and clear. It prioritised him in their pecking order. My brother was not much of a talker as in death and life. He accepted their disdain and tried to march on. We all have a fine line to the breaking point. Sometimes, people do not let us down. We have just held them in an incorrect esteem. How we walk with the broken speaks louder than how we sit with the great.

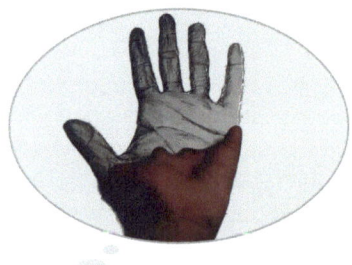

A disabled hand is not a silent cry! It is evidence for empathy, but society becomes tunnel visioned in the face of reality.

Image 4: A disabled hand with a sketch of the missing elements

Showing empathy to a person with a disabled hand is a meaningful way to support and connect with them. Start by treating them with the same respect and kindness you would offer anyone else. Be patient and understanding if they require more time for assistance with tasks. Avoid drawing unnecessary attention to their disability and avoid making unsolicited comments or questions about it. Instead, ask how you can be helpful and be willing to adapt your communication and actions to accommodate their needs. Most importantly, listen actively and show genuine interest in their experiences and feelings, allowing them to express themselves without judgement. Demonstrating empathy by being considerate and supportive goes a long way in making them feel valued and included.

There is always a space where we allow others to feel appreciated, seen, regarded, valued, heard, and loved, yet we rarely tap into this area proactively. Perhaps you can propose to connect over a chai date—some minutes of quiet listening. Having the bandwidth for intentional connection makes room for enjoyment, growth, tears, and the whole gamut that creates the fabric of life. It is the way someone greets us when we walk into a room or the way they hug us without rushing when we leave. It is helping a friend unravel their knots or holding a hand under a table. It is a thank you to the busiest cashier or sending a note about a kind medical provider. It is bringing dinner to a new mum, an exhausted parent, or making cookies for an elderly neighbour. It is extending a warm invitation to someone because you know how much being included will mean to them.

This space notices the good. The sweet spot is where the sun meets the sky and proclaims, "I'm glad you're here. I celebrate the gift of your presence." It is the opportunity presented to us, again and again, and our willingness to do better, to be better. And to value when others show up for us. The razor blade is sharp but cannot cut a tree, and the axe is strong but cannot cut hair. Morals! Everyone is important in accordance with his/her unique purpose. Connection facilitates hope. And hope is a seed for healing. Sadness is a solo gig. Therapy is a duet or chorus. Not all humans understand humanity.

"Listening to the silent cry" is a metaphorical expression that refers to understanding and empathising with someone suffering or in emotional pain, even if they are not explicitly expressing it or asking for help. It involves being attentive to subtle signs and signals, both verbal and non-verbal, that indicate distress or a need for support. In the context of suicide, listening to the silent cry means being aware of the signs of suicidal ideation and reaching out to assist. It involves paying attention to changes in behaviour, withdrawal from social interactions, expressions of hopelessness or despair, giving away belongings, or making alarming statements about self-harm or suicide. By actively listening and showing compassion, you may be able to identify individuals who are struggling and offer them the support they need. If you are concerned about someone's well-being or experiencing distress, it is crucial to seek help from a mental health professional, a helpline, or a trusted person. They can provide guidance, support, and resources to ensure the well-being and safety of those involved.

Are you part of the problem or the agent that can spot the drought and change in conditions? Do you have the intuition to discern what is brewing? Do you encourage open conversations about suicide and human welfare? How often do you practice the power of active listening and empathy? When have you created safe spaces for individuals to share their struggles? Are you proactive about building a supportive network? Microinequalities are small, everyday conscious and unconscious biases that substantially affect lives. Microaffirmations are small everyday gestures that make the recipient feel respected, included, and valued. You relate your meaning to a person by listening and responding. Are you a constant and defiant beacon of hope? Agape love is the glue that binds your mosaic. Adjust your outlook, challenge the powerful among us, and fortify the infirm.

Sometimes, it takes 30 years to get that one year that will change your life. Never give up. Re-set, re-adjust, re-start, and re-focus as often as needed. You get tested most when it is time for you to elevate. Do not allow the negative in others to break you. When you avoid difficult conversations, you trade short-term discomfort for long-term dysfunction. Yes, grow, but do not convince yourself that the past versions of you were worthless. You would not be here without them. Beautiful souls recognise beautiful souls. Keep being genuine. Your people will find you. If you could erase all the mistakes of your past, you would also remove the wisdom of the present. Remember the lesson, not the disappointment. When you throw out physical clutter, you clear your mind. When you toss out mental confusion, you will sharpen your life, and when you recognise people who do not value your welfare, it will liberate your soul. Fill your sails with acceptance and peace. This is the most joyous way to journey down the river of life.

It does not matter how others behave. What matters most is what you want to do despite all the odds that are stacked up against you. People will look down on you for all types of foolish reasons, both friends and family. Even though God commands us to love, people will mistreat others. Remember, hurting people hurt people. People can only behave as great as their evolution. Some have acquired money and qualifications but have no social grooming. Never subject yourself to unfortunate conduct. You are called to pray even for those who despitefully use you. With reference to the Bible, **"But I tell you, love your enemies and pray for those who persecute you." - Matthew 5:44.** People will always test and challenge you in every facet of life: in a relationship, professional liaison, personal connections, and international networks. People will shun you for many reasons. Remember, Christ was despised unto death. **"He was despised and rejected by mankind, a man of suffering and familiar with pain. Like one from whom people hide their faces, He was despised, and we held Him in low esteem." – Isaiah 53:3.** When you get over one challenge, the next one will be waiting for you.

In the Bible, the apostle Paul acknowledges that Timothy will face challenges in his ministry. Paul wrote two letters to Timothy, First Timothy, and Second Timothy, which provided guidance and encouragement to Timothy as a young leader in the early Christian church. While Paul acknowledged the difficulties Timothy would encounter, he also offered guidance on how Timothy should respond. Here are a few key points:

Perseverance: Paul encourages Timothy to persevere in his faith and not be discouraged by the challenges he faces. In 2 Timothy 1:7, Paul writes, **"For God has not given us a spirit of fear, but of power and of love and a sound mind."** Timothy is reminded to rely on God's strength and to trust in His provision.

Sound doctrine: Paul emphasises the importance of sound doctrine and teaching in Timothy's ministry. In 2 Timothy 4:2, Paul instructs Timothy to *"Preach the word; be prepared in season and out of season; correct, rebuke, and encourage—with great patience and careful instruction."* Timothy is encouraged to remain steadfast in his commitment to teaching the truth of the Gospel.

Endurance and faithfulness: Paul urges Timothy to endure hardships and remain faithful to his calling. In 2 Timothy 4:5, Paul writes, *"But you, keep your head in all situations, endure hardship, do the work of an evangelist, discharge all the duties of your ministry."* Timothy is reminded to stay focused, fulfil his responsibilities, and continue spreading the message of Christ despite any challenges.

Surrounding support: Paul highlights the importance of a supportive community. In 2 Timothy 2:2, he advises Timothy to entrust what he has learned to reliable people who will teach others. This encourages Timothy to seek out and build relationships with trustworthy individuals who will guide and support his ministry. In summary, Paul acknowledges the challenges Timothy will face but provides him with guidance on how to respond. Timothy is encouraged to persevere, teach sound doctrine, endure hardships, remain faithful, and seek support from a reliable community. These principles are intended to equip Timothy to face and overcome the challenges he encounters in his ministry. You can also adapt these principles to your personal life.

As you focus on clearing your generational trauma, do not forget to claim your generational strengths. Your ancestors gave you more than just wounds. Uncertainties are like raindrops that trickle down your windshield and stop you from seeing clearly. Keep your metaphoric windshield wipers on. Always remember that bees never waste their time explaining to flies why honey is better than shit. Never allow anyone to talk you out of your dreams. Control your thoughts when you are alone. Regulate your tongue when you are with friends. Recognise your decisions when you are angry. Pay attention to your behaviour when you sit in a group. Understand your pride when someone praises you. Acknowledge your emotions when someone wrongs you and respond rather than react.

Always elucidate your emotions before you act on them. Never allow the shadows of your past to darken the doorstep of your future. The most beautiful elements of one's character cannot be seen. It is found in your thoughts' measurements and your soul's serenity. Open your spirit to expand your discernment. Cry out for comprehension. Intercede for insight. Search the hidden places for cherished treasures. Seek to draw from the fountain of revelation and understanding. Access the hidden storehouse of wisdom. Choose what is right rather than what is easy. We all have baggage, no matter how much self-awareness we possess. Allow yourself some slack, as growth is a dance, not a switch. Is the problem really a problem? Most of the time, harm is caused by your perceived thoughts rather than the reality.

Refrain from self-rejection. The fact is most problems are not solved by more thinking. Most answers appear amid silence when you clear your mind. A critical question to ask yourself is, "Is there anything I can do right now to change the past to influence the future positively?" If the answer is yes, then take action. If the answer is no, find your peace and let it go. Make peace with yesterday, let go of tomorrow, and grab hold of the now—live in the power of now. It is important to always fact-check your thoughts before accepting them because, in highly emotional situations, your thoughts will tell you stories that are not true. You do not have to understand, tolerate, or even forget something, but if you seek peace, you must accept it. Peace will unravel in acceptance: accept imperfection, uncertainty, and the uncontrollable. Proper health is measured by the quality of your thoughts and the peacefulness of your mind. Health starts in your mind and is not measured on scales.

This paragraph is devoted to those who are struggling with their external image. The perception of attractiveness can vary from person to person, and there is no definitive measure or standard for attractiveness. However, it is not uncommon for individuals to perceive themselves differently from how others perceive them. Some studies suggest that people tend to view themselves less positively than others do, which can lead to a phenomenon known as the *"attractiveness gap."* It is important to note that attractiveness is subjective and influenced by various factors, including culture and personal preferences. Therefore, it is challenging to quantify attractiveness precisely. While it is natural for people to have self-perception biases, focusing on building a healthy self-image and self-esteem is essential. Remember that beauty is diverse, and everyone has unique qualities that make them attractive. It is important to value and appreciate yourself for who you are rather than comparing yourself to others or relying solely on external perceptions of attractiveness and validation.

It is difficult to turn the page when you know your loved one will never be in the next chapter, but the story must go on. Challenging misconceptions and reducing the stigma surrounding suicide is crucial to fostering a compassionate and supportive society. **"There is nothing noble in being superior to your fellow men. True nobility lies in being superior to your former self." – Ernest Hemingway.** The truth is not what you want it to be. It is what it is, and you must bend to its profound power or live a lie. By addressing these issues, we can promote understanding, help those in need, and ultimately save lives. Here are some key points to consider:

Open and honest dialogue: Encourage open conversations about suicide without judgement. Create a safe space where people feel comfortable discussing their thoughts, feelings, and experiences. This helps reduce stigma and promotes understanding.

Education and awareness: Raise awareness about suicide prevention, risk factors, and warning signs. Educate the public about the complexities of mental health issues and the various factors that contribute to suicidal thoughts. Dispelling myths and providing accurate information can help combat misconceptions.

Language matters: Choose your words carefully when discussing suicide. Avoid using sensationalised or judgmental language that may perpetuate stigma. Instead, use compassionate and non-stigmatizing language that emphasises empathy and understanding.

Sharing personal stories: Encourage individuals who have experienced suicidal thoughts or have been affected by suicide to share their stories if they are comfortable doing so. Personal narratives can help challenge stereotypes, provide hope, and let others know they are not alone.

Mental health support and resources: Advocate for accessible and affordable mental health resources, including counselling, therapy, and crisis helplines. Promote the importance of seeking help and emphasise that mental health conditions are treatable.

Responsible media reporting: Encourage responsible reporting of suicide-related incidents by the media. Journalists should adhere to guidelines that discourage explicit details, sensationalisation, or glamourisation of suicide. Accurate reporting and sensitive portrayal can prevent the spread of contagion and reduce stigma.

Training and education programs: Support the implementation of suicide prevention training programmes in schools, workplaces, and communities. These equip individuals with the knowledge and skills to identify warning signs, provide support, and connect people to appropriate resources.

Support for survivors: Recognise the unique needs of those who have lost a loved one to suicide. Provide support groups, counselling services, and resources to help survivors cope with their grief and navigate the complex emotions associated with suicide loss.

Collaboration and partnerships: Foster collaboration between mental health professionals, community organisations, government agencies, and individuals affected by suicide. Together, we can work towards destigmatizing suicide, promoting prevention, and supporting those in crisis.

Remember, challenging misconceptions and reducing the stigma surrounding suicide requires ongoing efforts from individuals, communities, and society. Promoting understanding, empathy, and support can create a more compassionate environment that values human welfare and saves lives. Screaming self-care at a fractured person who essentially requires community care is how we betray, forsake, and fail a person, a loved one. A disabled hand and unemployment are not silent cries, period. Disregard will slam doors shut, and regrets will never re-open. Making someone experience love, significance, and empathy is the richest way to love them.

"The three C's of life: Choices. Chances. Changes. You must make a choice to take a chance, or your life will never change." - Zig Ziglar.

5. Suicide Statistics: Let us Change the Narrative

During my sojourn to England, I visited the city of Bath. I am an avid traveller, and this city was nothing like I had experienced before. Pungent in history and architectural vistas, it is stuff that dreams are made off. Then I learned about the window tax. Yes, precisely. Bath, a city in England, did have a window tax during the 18th and 19th centuries. The window tax was a property tax based on the number of windows in a building. It was introduced in 1696 and remained in effect until 1851. The window tax was a way for the government to generate revenue. The more windows a building had, the higher the tax would be. This tax was particularly burdensome for those who lived in larger houses with many windows, such as mansions and townhouses.

Some homeowners decided to brick up or block off their windows to avoid paying higher taxes. By reducing the number of windows, they could lower their tax liability. As a result, you can still see many bricked-up windows in older buildings in Bath and other parts of the United Kingdom. The window tax had some unintended consequences. It decreased natural light inside buildings and created a gloomy atmosphere in many homes. The tax was eventually repealed in 1851 due to public opposition and the difficulty of enforcing it effectively. The bricked-up windows in Bath and other cities serve as a reminder of this historical tax and its impact on architecture and taxation during that period.

This history takes me to another end of the continuum. How we judge and tax humans unfairly eventually contributes to the statistics we must grapple with. Both conscious and unconscious biases create assumptions about people. This channels your behaviour towards a person. It determines whether you will help them in times of struggle or not. Whether you are in denial or not, we are all contributing to statistics daily. Suicide is a global public health issue that has significant social, emotional, and economic consequences. While it is a complex phenomenon influenced by various factors, including mental health, the social environment, and individual circumstances, understanding its statistics and global impact can provide valuable insights into the magnitude of the problem. Please note that the information provided below is based on data available until my research in July 2023, and the current statistics may have changed.

Global suicide rates: According to the World Health Organisation (WHO), approximately 800,000 people die by suicide each year. Suicide accounts for 1.4% of all deaths worldwide, making it the 17th leading cause of death globally. The global age-standardized suicide rate is estimated to be 10.5 per 100,000 people.

Regional variation: Suicide rates vary significantly across different regions and countries.

High-income countries: Generally have higher suicide rates than low-income countries, but this is not true in all cases. Some countries with particularly high suicide rates include Guyana, Lesotho, and Russia.

Age and gender patterns: Suicide rates tend to vary by age and gender. In many countries, suicide rates are higher among males than females. However, females tend to make more suicide attempts. The elderly population, particularly males, has elevated suicide rates in many countries, highlighting the importance of mental health support for older individuals.

Impact on mental health: Suicide has a significant impact on mental health and emotional well-being, both for individuals contemplating suicide and their families, friends, and communities. It is estimated that for each completed suicide, many more individuals have attempted suicide or have had suicidal thoughts. Suicide can contribute to a cycle of stigma, fear, and silence surrounding mental health issues.

Economic consequences: Suicide also has financial implications for societies. It can result in lost productivity, increased healthcare costs, and an overall burden on healthcare systems. Additionally, the emotional toll on families and communities affected by suicide can be substantial.

Prevention efforts: Suicide prevention is a critical public health priority. Many countries and organisations have implemented prevention strategies, including improving mental health services, raising awareness, reducing stigma, and promoting early identification and intervention.

Collaborative efforts are essential to address the complex factors contributing to suicide and provide support to those at risk. It is important to note that suicide is a sensitive topic, and if you or someone you know is struggling with suicidal thoughts, it is crucial to seek professional help immediately.

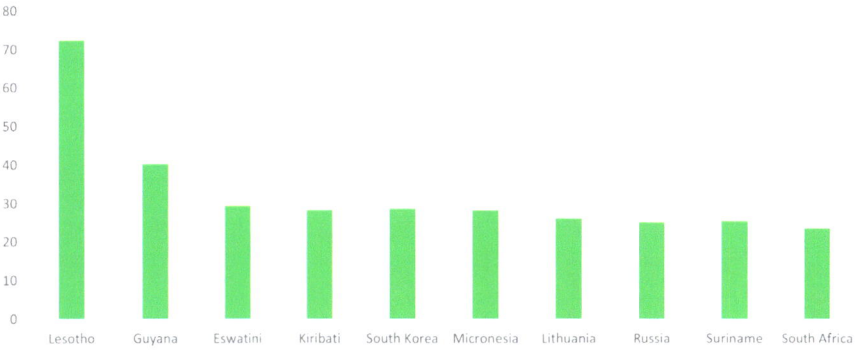

Image 5: Graph of suicide rates by country, data from World Health Organisation.

Disclaimer: In much of the world, suicide is stigmatized and condemned for religious or cultural reasons. In some countries suicide behaviour is a criminal offence punishable by law. Suicide is therefore often a secretive act surrounded by taboo, and may be unrecognized, misclassified or deliberately hidden in official records of death.

You deserve to be in an environment that brings out the best in you, not the survival in you. Never measure your progress using someone else's ruler. If you are feeling despondent, you are not alone. More than 65 million American adults experience clinically significant anxiety conditions at some point in their lives. Suicide has been documented since ancient times. Systematic research has been conducted for over 200 years. There are no universally agreed definitions of suicidal behaviour. Suicide explanation is bolstered by the 2007 publication of the book *Why People Die* by Suicide by Thomas Joiner, a clinical psychologist who is one of the world's most prominent and influential suicide researchers. According to the *interpersonal psychological theory*, suicidal desire and suicidal capability are necessary for suicide, but neither is sufficient on its own. In other words, wanting to kill oneself is not enough to die by suicide. One must also be able to do it. Likewise, possessing the ability to attempt suicide is not enough, and one must also want to die. The requirement for having both desire and capability provides a simple and easy-to-understand explanation for why suicide behaviour occurs so infrequently, even among individuals who are contemplating suicide.

There will be people who would rather lose you than be honest about what they have done to you. Purge before it is too late. Be brave enough to listen to the whisper of your soul instead of the roar of society. Remember, we all have positive and negative traits, and we all have some degree of toxic elements in us. Some people desire to be educated on it and do better, while others will ignore any trace of accountability and continue to act the same way. Pay attention to those who refuse to evolve. They are the stones that will drag you down. Life is the only thing that is truly yours. Refuse to feel guilty for wanting tranquility and quality. Acknowledging your triggers is not healing. Healing happens when you watch it and can move through the pain, the pattern, and the story and walk away to a different ending. You always have a choice at every moment, even if it feels like you do not. Sometimes, that choice may be to think a more positive thought.

Never forget that walking away from something or someone unhealthy is brave, even if you stumble a little on your way out of the door. Your direction is more important than your speed. If you become a master of your life, you learn how to control where your attention goes and how to value your time and energy. The privilege of a lifetime is to become who you are truly born to be. Life may not be the party you hoped for, but while you are here, you should dance in every season and bring your best vibes of life to the scene. The dandelion does not stop growing because it was told it was a weed. The dandelion does not care what others see. It says one day they will be making wishes via me. Take control of your destiny. Believe in yourself. Ignore those who will try to discourage you. Avoid negative sources, people, places, things, and habits. Never give up.

Those who love you will never hurt you in profound ways. We have been dying since birth. Remember to tune into life and smell the daily choices to live your finest life. Never decrease the goal. Always increase your effort. Dealing with setbacks requires wisdom to recognise, composure to handle, and tenacity to repair. People do not always need advice or money. Sometimes, all they need is a hand to hold, an ear to listen, an effort to wipe their tears, and a heart to understand. This does not need to be a big flame for all to see. It is just a tiny spark that softly whispers, keep going. You can do this. If you have to manipulate and hurt a disadvantaged person to acquire something in your own life, you are an extremely weak individual. When you cannot control what is happening around you, take a deep breath and challenge yourself to control how you react to it. That is where your power is. Behind every strong person is a story that does not give them any other choice.

Tough times can be a blessing in disguise. They always reveal the true colours of the people around us. Trust in the innocent is the liar's most useful tool. Life will always present challenges and problems. Learn to live life and enjoy it while you are solving them. Society will disrespect you regardless of whether you are at the top or bottom of the ladder. People will be dismissive, they will be envious, and oppressors will critique you as you discover things that liberate you. Stand strong. Just because you live a humble and modest life and do not require much does not equate to the fact that you deserve the bare minimum. Change the changeable, accept the unchangeable, and remove yourself from the unacceptable.

Patience is not just the ability to wait. It is the courage to endure the wait without losing hope. No matter how evolved a person is, they can only meet you as deeply as they have met and introspected themselves. Never make life choices based on someone else's behaviour.

I have learned that when sadness comes to visit me, I can only acknowledge it. I spend time dissecting the layers of pain, and I refrain from denial. I create a space to unravel its soaking presence and do the difficult milestones to accept it. I never push it away. Instead, I own it and then let it go. I then pray for a better tomorrow. Problems are part of life. Facing them is the art of life. Even if you are a hoarder of words, people will use them against you. Life is a craft. Growth is developing from a series of mistakes. Sometimes, you may have to sit sad and troubled, as life has no obligation to give us what we expect. This is not an invitation to give up. Rather, be patient. There is no magic formula. Life is difficult at the top. Just ponder how it is for someone with a disability and stripped of all confidence. With his dexterous skills despite his disability, Jayandra gave life a fair go until the statistics claimed him.

Changing the narrative around suicide statistics involves raising awareness, promoting understanding, and encouraging compassionate conversations. Here are some steps you can take to change the narrative:

Educate yourself: Learn about the complexities of suicide, mental health, and the factors that contribute to it. Familiarise yourself with reliable sources, such as mental health organisations, research institutions, and government agencies.

Use empathetic language: When discussing suicide, use compassionate and non-stigmatizing language. Avoid using judgmental or derogatory terms that can perpetuate negative stereotypes. Instead, emphasize the importance of empathy, understanding, and support.

Share accurate information: Challenge misconceptions and provide accurate information about suicide. Use statistics responsibly, ensuring that you cite credible sources and provide context to avoid misinterpretation. Promote awareness campaigns focusing on prevention, mental health resources, and support networks.

Highlight success stories: Shed light on stories of hope, resilience, and recovery from individuals who have experienced suicidal thoughts but found help and support. Sharing positive narratives can inspire others and reduce the stigma surrounding mental health challenges.

Encourage open conversations: Foster a supportive environment where people feel comfortable discussing mental health. Encourage dialogue about suicide prevention, warning signs, and available resources. Promote active listening and empathy, allowing individuals to express their feelings without judgment.

Collaborate with organizations: Partner with mental health organisations, community groups, and healthcare professionals to develop educational initiatives, awareness campaigns, and support networks. Working together can amplify efforts to change the narrative and reduce stigma.

Engage the media responsibly: Advocate for responsible reporting on suicide. Encourage journalists to follow established guidelines that prioritize sensitivity, avoid sensationalism, and provide helpful resources for those in need. Provide feedback to media outlets when you come across problematic or stigmatizing coverage.

Advocate for policy changes: Support policies that prioritize mental health services, suicide prevention programmes, and increased access to mental healthcare. Write to your local representatives, participate in awareness events, and join advocacy groups to raise your voice and influence change.

Remember, changing the narrative surrounding suicide statistics requires ongoing efforts and a collective commitment. It is essential to approach the topic with sensitivity, empathy, and a focus on prevention and support.

Never STOP just because you feel defeated. The journey to the next season is attainable only after great suffering and lessons learned. After your tears dry, and eventually they will, your vision will become clear. Let a clarifying spark emerge from the darkness. Delve deep to find yourself: maybe bruised, traumatised, fragmented, battered and bare, stripped of every comfort but clothed in the naked truths. Begin to bloom in the once shattered places purposefully, rather than crawling down an emotional rabbit hole of despair. You believe in the sun, even when it does not shine. You believe in love, even when you feel alone. Believe in God, even if He is silent. This is your path to victory. Live this audacious life with tenacity.

A country flag does not fly because of the wind. It flies with the last breath of each soldier who died protecting it. Similarly, a person exists and lives abundantly when every family member protects and supports a person in that family tree. Empathy is born out of compassion. How can you live a life in the valley of despair and not have any empathy or compassion for someone who has killed themselves in your own family, community, or world? We can all change the narrative and the statistics.

How to Talk to a Suicidal Person

Be there when people need you. Offer care and compassion as a sacred encounter with transformative potential. Take a holistic approach to the human condition that values lives.

Invest in relationships that promote mutual flourishing. Tackle the social systems that harm creation and strip away human dignity. Educate yourself on how to talk to someone distressed and suicidal. Polish your skills with empathy, patience, and a supportive approach. Here are some steps to help you communicate effectively with someone who is going through a difficult time:

Create a safe and comfortable environment: Find a quiet and private place to talk without distractions. Ensure that the person feels physically and emotionally safe.

Stay calm: Remain composed and nonjudgmental. Show empathy and understanding.

Listen actively: Pay full attention to the person and put aside your thoughts and judgements. Maintain eye contact and use nonverbal cues, like nodding, to show engagement.

Ask about safety: Gently ask if they have a plan, means, and intent to harm themselves. This will help you assess the level of risk.

Stay with them: If possible, stay with them or keep them on the line. Offer support and let them know they are not alone.

Empathise and validate feelings: Acknowledge the person's emotions without judgment. You can say things like, "I can see that you're upset right now," or "It's okay to feel this way."

Use open-ended questions: Encourage them to talk by asking open-ended questions like, "Can you tell me more about what's bothering you?" or "How has this been affecting you?"

Reflect their feelings: Reflecting their emotions on them can help them feel heard. For example, "It sounds like you're feeling overwhelmed by this situation."

Avoid offering immediate solutions: Unless they specifically ask for advice, it is often better to listen and empathize rather than try to solve their problems immediately.

Offer support and reassurance: Let them know that you are there for them and that they can count on you for support. You can say things like, "I'm here to listen." or "You're not alone in this."

Avoid judgment and criticism: Refrain from passing judgment or making critical comments about their situation or feelings.

Respect their boundaries: If the person does not want to talk or needs space, respect their wishes, and let them know you are available whenever they're ready.

Suggest professional help if needed: If you believe the person's distress is severe or if they mention thoughts of self-harm or suicide, encourage them to seek professional help immediately. Offer to assist them in finding a therapist, counsellor, or crisis hotline.

Contact emergency services: If the situation is immediate and severe, do not hesitate to contact emergency services or a crisis hotline.

Avoid keeping secrets: If the risk is high, consider involving a trusted friend, family member, or mental health professional.

Do not minimise their feelings: Avoid telling them to "snap out of it" or minimizing their pain. Take their words seriously.

Express concern: Let them know you care about their well-being. Say something like, "I'm really worried about you and want to help."

Involve trusted individuals: If the risk is high, consider involving a trusted friend or family member who can provide additional support.

Follow up: After the initial conversation, check in with them later to see how they are doing. Let them know that you care and are still there to support them.

Remember, talking to someone who is suicidal can be emotionally challenging. It is important to prioritize their safety and well-being by involving professionals if required.

Remember that every individual is different, and what works for one person may not work for another. The key is to be compassionate, nonjudgmental, and willing to adapt your approach based on the person's needs. If you are unsure how to handle a specific situation, it is always a good idea to seek guidance from a mental health professional or counsellor.

As you grapple with the aftermath of suicide, equip yourself with knowledge. Know the facts on suicide:

~~People who talk about killing themselves will not do it.~~

If someone talks about it, always take them seriously.

~~There are no warning signs.~~

According to statistics, 8 out of 10 people have given definite warnings.

~~Young people are more likely than old people to kill themselves.~~

Statistics reveal that people 65 and older kill themselves at a higher rate than those who are aged 15-24.

~~Don't place your mistakes on your head, the weight may crush you.~~

Instead, place them under your feet as steppingstones to view your future horizons.

According to Centers of Disease Control and Prevention (CDC) - suicide is a serious public health problem:

- ♦ Suicide is a leading cause of death in the USA. It was responsible for over 48,000 deaths in 2021, which is about one death every 11 minutes.
- ♦ In 2021 the USA estimated 12.3 million adults seriously thought about suicide, 3.5 million made a plan and 1.7 million attempted suicide.
- ♦ Provisional 2022 data show that suicide deaths increased by 2.6% between 2021 - 2022.

"Mishandling people, then avoiding communication, is not protecting your peace. It is avoiding accountability." - Unknown.

6. The Kernel of Life

The phrases *"kernel of life"* and *"essence of life"* refer to the fundamental or core aspects crucial for life to exist and thrive. While these terms are not scientific concepts with specific definitions, they often carry philosophical, spiritual, or metaphorical meanings:

- ♦ Kernel of life: In this context, *"kernel"* implies the central, essential part of the seed from which life originates and grows. It can be seen as the basic building block or vital principle that underlies all living organisms. Different cultures and belief systems may attribute different meanings to the *"kernel of life,"* ranging from biological explanations to more abstract or mystical interpretations.

- ♦ Essence of life: The *"essence"* refers to the intrinsic nature or defining characteristic that makes something what it is. The *"essence of life"* is the fundamental principle distinguishing living beings from non-living matter. Philosophically, it may refer to the underlying force that drives and sustains life or the essence that gives life its purpose and meaning.

Overall, both phrases evoke the idea that life possesses a core element or principle that sets it apart and enables its existence. However, the specific interpretation of these concepts can vary widely depending on cultural, religious, and philosophical perspectives. In addition, each person has their values and outlook on life. We all value and prioritise different things. We are all human beings. We take the wrong turns, and we make mistakes. Some of us make amends, and we grow. While others do not move beyond regrets and disappointment, they never did well in the warm light of self-forgiveness and a simple apology. The most beautiful people I have encountered have nothing to do with their appearance or status. It has everything to do with how they make people feel. You always pass failure on your way to success. Your willingness to look at your darkness is what empowers you to change. Sometimes, we treat life as a race to finish when it is just a walk. The moments become the best memories of life at the worst.

The spirit of *"Ubuntu"* is a philosophical concept that originates from Southern Africa, particularly among the Bantu people, and has been popularized in various contexts, including within the open-source software community and general philosophy. Ubuntu is an ancient Nguni Bantu term meaning *"humanity towards others"* or *"I am because we are."* It embodies the ideas of interconnectedness, compassion, and communal values. The philosophy emphasizes the belief that our well-being and happiness are closely tied to the well-being and happiness of others. It is often described as a way of life or an ethic rather than a specific doctrine or set of rules. Ubuntu emphasizes the value of relationships and encourages individuals to act in ways that promote the well-being of the community. At its most basic level, ubuntu is about recognizing the humanity in others and treating them with respect and dignity. It is about acknowledging that our well-being is intimately tied to the well-being of others and that we cannot thrive as individuals unless our community is healthy and prosperous. It encourages cooperation, empathy, and mutual support among individuals and communities. The spirit of Ubuntu can be summarized by the following principles:

Interconnectedness: Recognizing that we are all interconnected and that our actions affect others in the community.

Compassion: Showing empathy and care for others, acknowledging their struggles, and offering help when needed.

Cooperation: Working together for the greater good, understanding that collective efforts can lead to more significant achievements.

Respect: Respecting the dignity and worth of every individual, regardless of their background or status.

Sharing: Being generous and willing to share resources and knowledge with others.

Forgiveness: Acknowledging that everyone makes mistakes and embracing a forgiving and understanding attitude.

One of the most famous expressions of ubuntu comes from Archbishop Desmond Tutu, who described it as follows: *"A person with ubuntu is open and available to others, affirming of others, does not feel threatened that others are able and good, for he or she has a proper self-assurance that comes from knowing that he or she belongs in a greater whole and is diminished when others are humiliated or diminished when others are tortured or oppressed."* This definition captures the essence of ubuntu, which is all about interconnectedness and the recognition that our actions can profoundly impact others. It encourages us to act with kindness, compassion, and empathy and work towards creating a world where everyone can thrive.

Ubuntu is often contrasted with individualism, which emphasizes the importance of personal freedom and autonomy. While individualism has its benefits, ubuntu reminds us that we are not solitary creatures but social beings who need connection and community to thrive. It encourages us to think beyond ourselves and to consider the needs and desires of others. Ubuntu has been used to guide social and political movements in Africa, particularly during the struggle against apartheid in South Africa. It has also influenced the development of restorative justice practices, emphasising the importance of repairing harm and restoring relationships rather than simply punishing offenders. Ubuntu is a powerful philosophy that emphasises the importance of community, compassion, and empathy. It reminds us that we are all interconnected and that our actions can profoundly impact others. By embracing ubuntu, we can work towards creating a more just and equitable world where everyone can thrive.

Ubuntu is not just a concept; it is a way of life that shapes interpersonal relationships, societal structures, and decision-making within communities. By embracing the spirit of Ubuntu, individuals can foster a sense of belonging, social cohesion, and harmony among diverse groups. Nelson Mandela often referenced ubuntu in his speeches and writings, helping to popularize the concept globally as a symbol of unity, reconciliation, and peace. How do you practice the spirit of ubuntu? *"The child who is not embraced by the village will burn it down to feel its warmth." - African proverb.* Life can be harsh at the best of times, and we all need support and a healthy network to sustain us through the valleys of life. No one can survive or thrive in isolation. Today is the day you can change the narrative for people struggling with unseen trauma. The person who watch others drown is no different than the person who holds your head beneath the water. Inaction is just as evil as action. Become proactive with your ubuntu spirit.

Choose resolution instead of comfort, decide what is edifying rather than following the fad, be dependable rather than treacherous, and elect to practice your values rather than simply advertising them. Become a peacemaker rather than a peacekeeper.

Image 6: The missing piece

Practice creating a favourite extreme sport for being an empath in society. This may be the last piece of the puzzle in someone's life. Your empathy could show them a brighter future, give them hope, and prevent suicide. When you spill your drink, and someone asks you why you spilt your coffee, most respond with the default that it was a mistake, or someone bumped them. Another option is that the cup was filled with coffee, so it spilt; if it was filled with tea, tea would spill out. The same analogy is applicable to life. What overflows out of you by default when someone rubs you up the wrong way? Undoubtedly, the contents will always come rushing to the surface. This could be in peace, love, understanding, patience, humility, anger, vengeance, wickedness, or evil. What is rooted and growing in your heart will most definitely spill out in the commotion of life.

Jayandra did not have people. He was the person that society had. Jayandra painted the sky, saying that he refused to burn the village again to feel its warmth:

1. No one should be pushed to obtain what legally belongs to them.
2. Bend the truth to make someone else feel comfortable.
3. Apologise for setting a boundary.
4. Sometimes, you must make a decision that will break your heart but give peace to your soul.

Never be pushed by your problems. Be led by your dreams. Allow your dreams to steer the way. Align yourself to push past your problems and permit your dreams to lead the way as your guiding stars. Let it illuminate a path for you even in dark times. Remember, obstacles are temporary, but the power of your dream is everlasting. God knows this season has brought more rain than sunshine into your life. He understands that you are overwhelmed and overlooked. Always remember that nothing grows in sunshine alone. Every season matters. He is sowing something beautiful through all this experience. Trust Him for a great harvest. Become so healed that the only thing that can trigger you is the phoenix within. Learn to differentiate between the sound of your intuition guiding you and your trauma misleading you. The two most important days of your life are when you were born, and the day you discovered why. Everything in between is your opportunity. Your nervous system will naturally feel calm around people with pure intentions and authentic energy. Trust it.

Never be offended when people start leaving your life. A season of loss always happens before great growth. Focus. Their exit is prophetic. When your next level approaches, the negative forces will attack you through people you thought loved you. They open themselves up as vessels of bitterness and betrayal. Overcome this by remaining focused and keeping your eye on the goal. Shifts are mandatory. They must happen so that we can continue to grow. This shift is like pruning. God is shifting you to a new position for the next level of blessings. You cannot go into a new place with God with out-of-season old friends and family. Although it hurts and you will miss them, you must hold onto what is necessary for the next level in the new season. Do not try to take unauthorised people who are not assigned to your future. Let them go. The purge is necessary. Relationships are like seatbelts. If they do not click, you will never be safe. **"Sometimes God slows you down so that the evil ahead of you will pass before you get there. Your delay could mean your protection." - Mark Wahlberg.**

Establish goals so that you develop the spiritual stamina to combat problems when they occur. React out of wisdom rather than emotion. There are some pieces of life that only you can fill, and no one else can. There are some things in life that only you and no one else can do. Realise that you are one of a kind, crafted by God for a purpose. Find your purpose and live it out loud. The truth is you had a purpose before anyone had an opinion. Finish your mission. Change is inevitable. How you react or respond to it will make all the difference. Embrace what is being dished out, even if it is an unfair shake. Your emotions and character will eventually catch up with your heart and sparkle with a new trait. It is good when permission is given to experience freedom instead of being a jailbird, especially in the face of adversity. In most cases, you must invent freedom. Freedom is defined by the puppet strings that you permit not to control you.

Not every opinion matters, and not every person deserves a seat at your table, even if they are related to you. Emotional intelligence is about being intentional with the opinions you let into your life and allow to influence you. Not all advice deserves to be taken. Always consider the source. This is a crucial part of the process. Everyone has an opinion and an agenda. Ensure it aligns with your vision and values. Understand when the snake enters the chicken coop. Surround yourself with a network of people who have your best interests at heart and have proven that they are for you. Past behaviour is a good predictor of future behaviour, which is a great yardstick to measure people's intentions. Also, understand the power of the undercurrent at play. The matriarchal spirit always wreaks havoc and refrains from disregarding it. Envy, in all simplicity, can sink a ship. Be acutely aware of how people will use others around you to bring you down or affect you and your loved ones adversely. Surround yourself with people willing to speak the truth and create an authentic circle of value, mutual empowerment, growth, and enhancement. Be part of a culture that helps you find answers; if they do not have the answer, they will leave no stone unturned to obtain one for you.

"Unsavoury characters" is a colloquial expression used to refer to individuals considered morally questionable, disreputable, or involved in activities that are frowned upon by society. These individuals might engage in unethical, illegal, or socially unacceptable behaviours. The term "unsavoury" suggests that these characters are distasteful or unpleasant in some way. Be aware of unsavoury characters:

1. Some people did not die when the arrow hit their chest. They died when they saw who threw the arrow.

2. Nasty people plot against you at night and laugh with you in the morning
3. They appear when they need you and disappear when you need them the most
4. Your success threatens them
5. Indulging in emotional blackmail is their favourite pastime
6. They are always competitive
7. Average minds focus on the negative rather than fostering the positive
8. They constantly discredit you and your worth
9. They are inconsistent and not trustworthy
10. The insalubrious have no remorse for hurting you and make no effort to apologise
11. The unpleasant rejoices when something unfortunate happens to you

A problem shared is a problem halved, suggesting that when you share your issues or concerns with someone else, sharing itself can alleviate some of the burdens you feel. By discussing your worries, you may find emotional relief and potentially gain new perspectives or insights on how to address the issue. This saying underscores the idea that keeping problems bottled up can contribute to increased stress and anxiety, while sharing them with a friend, family member, therapist, or counsellor can provide a sense of relief and help you approach the problem with a clearer mind. While sharing a problem may not necessarily reduce its complexity or difficulty, sharing can lighten the emotional load and potentially lead to collaborative problem-solving or emotional support from others. The fundamental focus is to share your problems with the right person. Remember, the unsavoury character does not have your best interests at heart. You need to seek out your authentic support group. Your decisions, not your conditions, determine your destiny. Make wise choices. You never lose people in life. However, you re-evaluate your energy and synergy and realign with those in harmony with you.

If you see someone falling behind, walk beside them. If you see someone being ignored, find a way to include them. Always remind people of their value. One small gesture could mean the world to them, and it could mean the difference between life and death. Life is an experience, not a statistic. Create a landscape for humans to live out their experiences. Every person wants to be accepted on their terms and to understand and respect their boundaries. You must defeat your enemies to save lives. When you make someone feel unworthy, they will be riddled with shame. You must be sure about where you are going, regardless of the moral corrosion around you. Always be armed for the bear. Show up for life with enough buttress. It will keep you breathing. *"If you hear the dogs, keep going. If you see the torches in the woods, keep going. If there is shouting after you, keep going. Don't ever stop. Keep going. If you want a taste of freedom, keep going." – Harriet Tubman.* It will take courage to keep going:

Physical courage: To keep going with resilience, balance, and awareness

Social courage: To be yourself unapologetically

Moral courage: Doing the right thing even when it is uncomfortable or unpopular

Emotional courage: Feeling all your emotions, positive and negative, without guilt or attachment

Intellectual courage: To learn, unlearn, and relearn with an open and flexible mind

Spiritual courage: Living with purpose and meaning through a heart-centred approach towards all and oneself

The truth cannot be seen but felt with the heart. Family and friendships are built on trust. You cannot get there on suspicion. The self-righteous will scream judgment against you to hide the noise of skeletons dancing in your closet. Our worst times define us, but we never allow them to confine us. Some people are eager to destroy you, and they will find your survival offensive. You cannot flourish with people who do not appreciate how growth looks on you. Sometimes, you win, and occasionally you may lose. Losing can be a win in a different facet when the lesson is gleaned from the loss. And you forge forward with richer lived experience, better equipped.

"Getting over a painful experience is much like crossing monkey bars. You have to let go at some point in order to move forward." - C.S Lewis.

7. Suicide Prevention in the Technology Age

Thankfully, Jayandra did not subscribe to the hype of social media. He was not on any platforms or group chats. He embraced life in all its simplicity. Suicide prevention in the digital age is a critical and complex challenge due to the increasing reliance on technology and social media. The internet and social platforms can be both beneficial and harmful in addressing human welfare concerns, including suicide risk. Here are some key aspects and strategies for suicide prevention in the digital age:

Mental health awareness and education: Promote mental health awareness and education on digital platforms. Encourage open discussions about mental health, suicide, and available resources to reduce the stigma surrounding these issues.

Safe online spaces: Create and maintain safe online spaces where individuals can discuss their struggles without fear of judgement or harassment. Moderation and intervention may be necessary to prevent harmful interactions.

Monitoring social media platforms: Collaborate with social media companies to identify and respond to potentially suicidal content or expressions. Employ algorithms and human moderators to detect and remove harmful content promptly.

Artificial Intelligence (AI) and machine learning: Utilize AI and machine learning algorithms to identify patterns of behaviour associated with suicidal ideation, allowing for early intervention and support.

Crisis helplines and chatbots: Implement crisis helplines and AI-powered chatbots that can provide immediate support to distressed individuals, offering resources, and connecting them to professional help.

Online counselling and therapy: Make online counselling and therapy services accessible and affordable for individuals who may not have easy access to in-person mental health support.

Training for moderators and staff: Train social media platform moderators and staff on identifying signs of distress and self-harm, enabling them to respond appropriately and direct users to appropriate resources.

Geolocation and reporting tools: Develop geolocation tools to identify users who may be at risk and send immediate help or contact local authorities in emergency situations.

Collaboration with mental health organizations: Partner with mental health organisations and crisis centres to provide resources and support for those at risk.

Limiting access to harmful content: Restrict access to content that promotes self-harm or suicide and encourage responsible media reporting on suicide cases to avoid copycat incidents.

Promotion of resilience and coping strategies: Emphasise the importance of resilience, coping strategies, and self-care in digital campaigns and platforms.

Parental controls and education: Educate parents and guardians about the risks associated with the digital world and encourage them to utilize parental controls and monitoring tools.

Data privacy and ethics: Maintain strong data privacy policies and ethical guidelines when dealing with sensitive mental health information.

Peer support networks: Foster online peer support networks that allow individuals to connect with others who have experienced similar challenges and encourage a sense of belonging.

Long-term follow-up: Ensure ongoing support and follow-up for individuals who have expressed suicidal thoughts or engaged with suicide prevention resources online.

Remember that suicide prevention in the digital age requires a multi-faceted approach involving cooperation between technology companies, mental health professionals, policymakers, and users themselves. Digital platforms create a vortex in an already challenging world. Some users get trapped in a cage of comparison, envy, covertness, condemnation, bullying, jealousy, pretense, gas lighting, and so on. The online virtual world has created a sense of profound jealousy when people look at the status of others, regardless of whether it delivers any element of truth or not. People feel adequate when they are exposed to others who are achieving. Some feel resentment rather than celebrating the wins of others.

Why?

Shift your focus and zoom into your life. Create your status upgrade. Become the better person that you were yesterday. We are all in our lanes. Life is not a competition, and your value does not equate to the number of followers or likes you obtain. Digital platforms are verbose and loquacious, and even those with the gift of the gab struggle to keep up. Understand that this is a virtual environment and not the real world. Take things with a pinch of salt. I am an international award-winning and bestselling author. I have an active digital media profile. And those who profess to be my friends, collaborating with and supporting me, do not always express positive vibrations. I have discerned to pay attention to the unspoken, unexpressed, and expressed. I know precisely who is for me and who is bringing surveillance cameras into my life. This, however, does not derail my vision and purpose. I use digital media as a tool, and I do not permit it to control my outcomes and emotions. ***"Your imagination is your preview of the life's coming attractions." – Albert Einstein.***

It is not uncommon for celebrities and individuals alike to express that their lives have improved after stepping away from or reducing their use of social media. General insights into why some people may feel this way:

Reduced stress and pressure: Social media platforms can be overwhelming, particularly for celebrities, who often face intense scrutiny and criticism from the public. By distancing themselves from social media, they can avoid negative comments and the constant pressure to present a curated image.

Increased privacy: Social media blurs the line between public and private life. Celebrities who step away from these platforms can regain some control over their personal spaces and experiences.

Improved mental health: Social media can lead to feelings of inadequacy, jealousy, and anxiety when comparing one's life to others. By disengaging from these platforms, individuals may experience improved mental well-being and a more positive outlook.

Enhanced Focus on Real-Life Interactions: Without the distraction of social media, celebrities can focus more on their personal relationships, projects, and daily activities.

Time management: Social media can be addictive, consuming significant time. Individuals may find more time to engage in meaningful pursuits and hobbies by quitting or reducing usage.

Freedom from online drama: Social media can be a breeding ground for conflicts, rumours, and controversies. By avoiding it, celebrities can escape unnecessary drama and maintain a peaceful existence.

The impact of social media varies from person to person, and not everyone may experience the same benefits or drawbacks. It is essential to remember that while social media has its advantages, it also comes with challenges and potential adverse effects. Business intelligence has given us the edge with technology. We can use this to our advantage rather than our demise. *"World Uncertainty Index"* has served as a universally recognized global measurement. Some organizations and research institutions have published various indices or measurements related to global uncertainty. These indices aimed to quantify the level of uncertainty in the world's economic, geopolitical, and social conditions. Keep in mind that data changes with the progression of time, and new metrics may have emerged since my research.

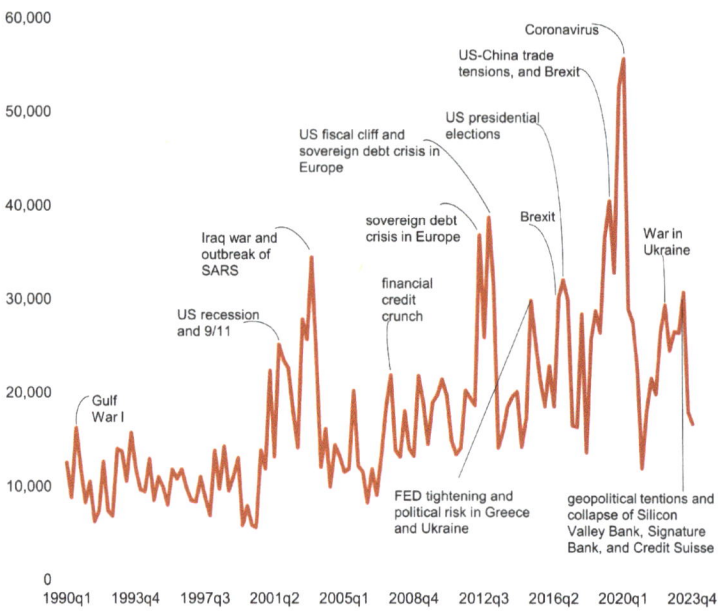

Image 7: Data of the "World Uncertainty Index" 1990Q1 to 2023Q4

The World Uncertainty Index is a measure that tracks uncertainty across the globe by text-mining the country reports of the Economist Intelligence Unit. The index is available for 143 countries. The WUI is computed by counting the percentage of the word *"uncertain"* (or its variant) in the Economist Intelligence Unit country reports. The WUI is then rescaled by multiplying by 1,000,000. A higher number means higher uncertainty, and vice versa.

The fact that we have a report that gives us global intelligence on uncertainty is alarming enough. This denotes that our world is smothered in uncertainty. There are factors in the world and in life that are uncertain and, thus, may be out of your control. Uncertainty is an inherent aspect of life; many factors can be beyond your control. Here are some examples of areas where uncertainty and a lack of control can exist:

Natural events: Natural disasters like earthquakes, hurricanes, floods, pandemics, and wildfires are unpredictable and can significantly impact our lives.

Economic conditions: Economic fluctuations, recessions, or market crashes are beyond individual control but can affect personal financial stability.

Health and illness: Despite caring for our health, we cannot always predict or prevent illnesses or accidents.

Other people's actions: You cannot control the decisions and actions of others, and sometimes those actions might have consequences for us.

Technological advancements: Rapid technological advancements can lead to uncertainties in job markets and industries.

Political and social changes: Societal and political developments can create uncertainties about laws, regulations, and policies that may impact our lives.

Relationships: Interactions with others involve uncertainties and sometimes unexpected outcomes.

Personal circumstances: Life can throw unexpected challenges or opportunities, like sudden job changes or relocations.

Weather: Weather conditions can change unexpectedly, affecting travel plans and outdoor activities.

Future events: No one can accurately predict what will happen, making life uncertain.

We all have elements of uncertainty in life. There are no guarantees in life apart from taxes and death. The road to rediscovery is the key in uncertain times. Look for ways to adapt rather than give up. Chart a path towards recovery and healing. Develop coping mechanisms and self-care strategies. Build a life worth living. Imagine the future after all the uncertainty thrown your way. "The *Ripple Effect*" is a metaphor often used to describe how a single action or event can have far-reaching consequences, spreading out like ripples in water and affecting other people and situations beyond its immediate scope. The concept is commonly used in various fields, including physics, social sciences, and philosophy, to illustrate the interconnectedness and interdependence of different elements within a system. In physics, the *Ripple Effect* can be seen in the propagation of waves. When a stone is dropped into a still pond, it creates a series of concentric circles that expand outward from the point of impact. Each circle represents a wave of energy travelling through the water. These waves spread, affecting the surrounding water and objects in their path.

In a social context, the *ripple effect can be observed in how actions and behaviours* influence others. For example, a small act of kindness towards someone might inspire that person to do something kind for someone else, creating a chain reaction of positive actions. Conversely, negative actions can also lead to a chain reaction of negative consequences.

The *Ripple Effect* can be seen in broader contexts as well. For instance, in economics, a change in one sector of the economy can have widespread impacts on other sectors and even across countries. In environmental science, a single ecological disturbance can create cascading effects on the entire ecosystem.

The concept of the *Ripple Effect* reminds us that our actions and decisions can have profound and far-reaching implications beyond what we might initially realize. It underscores the importance of considering the potential consequences of our actions and making choices that promote positive outcomes for individuals and society. Additionally, it emphasizes the interconnectedness of all things, highlighting the need for holistic and systemic thinking in addressing complex problems. While we cannot eliminate uncertainty, we can develop coping strategies to deal with it better by:

Adaptability: Cultivate adaptability to navigate uncertain situations and be open to change.

Resilience: Strengthen your resilience to bounce back from challenges and setbacks.

Planning and preparation: While we cannot control everything, being prepared and having contingency plans can help manage uncertainties.

Focus on what you can control: Concentrate on the aspects of life you can influence, such as your attitude, actions, and decisions.

Seek support: During uncertain times, lean on your support system—friends, family, or professionals.

Mindfulness: Practice mindfulness to stay grounded and present during uncertain situations.

Learn and grow: Embrace uncertainty as an opportunity to learn and develop new skills.

Remember, uncertainty is a part of life, and it is essential to find a balance between accepting what we cannot control and taking action in the areas we can influence. Life has barely bloomed for some, yet it has come to a grinding halt. Despite all the technological advancements, we still display primitive behaviour in our current landscape. Strive to impact lives in a small but significant way. Learn how to administer balms to beating hearts. We all want to enjoy our time on earth with serenity. It is not a tall ask to help another person achieve that. Resolutely, never live with regrets. Never procrastinate with intentions. It may be too late for someone grappling with life and death. And then it is often too late. The right time is now. Make a material difference right now. Our environment plays a significant role in shaping narratives in several ways:

Cultural and social influence: The culture and society an individual grows up in heavily influence their beliefs, values, and worldview. These factors shape the narratives they are exposed to and contribute to the stories they tell themselves and others. Cultural narratives can vary widely across different societies and impact how people perceive events, history, social issues, and themselves. Be strategic about what you allow to influence you.

Personal experiences: Personal experiences within their environment can shape their narrative. Positive or negative experiences can influence how individuals perceive the world and construct their own stories. For example, someone who has experienced trauma may develop a different narrative compared to someone who has lived a more privileged life.

Media and information sources: The information individuals consume, such as news, books, movies, and social media, can shape their narratives. Different media outlets and sources may present information with various biases and perspectives, influencing how people interpret events and form their narratives about the world.

Economic status: Socioeconomic factors can impact people's narratives, as individuals from different economic backgrounds may face other challenges, opportunities, and perspectives on life. Economic inequality can lead to divergent narratives on issues like poverty, social justice, and the role of government.

Political climate: The political environment can heavily influence people's narratives. Political leaders and parties often craft narratives to support their agendas, and these narratives can shape public opinion and belief systems.

Historical context: A society's historical events and collective memory play a role in shaping its narrative. How a country or community interprets its past can significantly impact its identity and how it views current events and future possibilities.

Education and education systems: An individual's education can influence their narrative by providing them with certain knowledge, perspectives, and critical thinking skills. The education system may also promote certain narratives about history, science, culture, and societal norms.

It is essential to recognise that narratives are not always precise representations of reality; they are often subjective interpretations influenced by various environmental factors. Awareness of these influences can help individuals critically assess their narratives and be more open to understanding alternative perspectives. In a broader sense, understanding how your environment affects narratives is essential for promoting empathy, inclusivity, and constructive dialogue in society. You have survived too many storms to be bothered by raindrops; get your perspective on the right track. Understand how your character is bankrupted when you allow technology or anything else to steal the narrative. It is fascinating how life keeps testing your balance. Keep passing the test that life presents, and you will see new levels of your destiny. When you are worried, anxious, and perplexed while life meanders through more roadblocks than roads, find the source that feeds the soul.

In the whirlwind of our hectic lives, it is easy to overlook the power of gratitude. Yet, during these frantic moments, pausing to acknowledge our blessings can be most transformative. Gratitude is an anchor, grounding us in the present and reminding us of the beauty amid the chaos. It allows us to appreciate the small joys, the kindness of others, and the simple wonders that often go unnoticed. Amid the commotion, practising gratitude can be a source of solace and strength, reminding us that even in the disarray of life, there is much to be thankful for, and this alone can bring a sense of peace and balance to our lives.

Appreciate the fact that you are blessed with the gift of life. Many have their lives cut short and leave without saying goodbye sometimes. Be grateful that you have a mind that allows you to experience life profoundly. Be thankful for your eyes, which permit you to see the beauty in life and the faces of your loved ones. Value your healthy body, which serves you in beautiful ways. Be thankful to the people who have shown up for you and those who have made sacrifices for you. Be grateful that you have life. This is the greatest miracle of all. Forgive yourself for your past mistakes and the lessons learned to improve your future.

Ten lessons to remember in difficult times:

1. You are capable of more than you can fathom
2. Most of what you think truly matters
3. Your greatest asset is the present moment
4. You are not the only one facing struggle
5. Always zoom into your blessings
6. Authentic family and friends are priceless
7. Use every experience to enhance yourself
8. Understand that no suffering is forever
9. You are never alone
10. Kindness and mercy are free

Bonus:

Your current misery does not define you; it certainly can refine you.

"Unexpressed emotions will never die. They are buried alive and will come back later in uglier ways." - Sigmund Freud.

Smoothie Recipe

Ayurvedic medicine offers holistic approaches to mental health, including diet and lifestyle recommendations. While it does not provide specific "smoothie recipes" for depression, it does emphasize balancing your doshas (Vata, Pitta, and Kapha) and consuming foods that promote mental well-being. A general Ayurvedic approach to supporting mental health might include:

- Warm and grounding ingredients: Use cooked oats, bananas, almonds, and dates.
- Herbs and spices: Incorporate ingredients like ashwagandha, turmeric, and cardamom for their potential mood-boosting properties.
- Healthy fats: Include ghee or coconut oil for brain health.
- Avoid processed foods, caffeine, and excessive sugar, which can exacerbate imbalances.

Remember that Ayurveda is highly individualized, so it is best to consult an Ayurvedic practitioner who can assess your specific constitution and recommend personalized dietary changes to support your mental well-being.

This recipe is inspired by an Ayurvedic Ojas shake. Both dates and almonds help to restore your ojas, leaving you feeling balanced and grounded.

- Four pitted dates
- A handful of almonds
- ¼ teaspoon of cardamom powder
- ¼ teaspoon of turmeric powder
- One banana
- Two teaspoons of honey

Blend all the ingredients in the blender until smooth. It is excellent to have in the morning and evening.

8. Residues Before and After Suicide

The kookaburra birds are native to Australia and are known for their distinctive call, which sounds like a loud, echoing laughter. Their call is often described as *"kook-kook-kook-kaa-kaa-kaa"* or *"koo-koo-koo-koo-koo-kaa-kaa-kaa."* The sound is quite recognizable and is a unique feature of these birds. Kookaburras are part of the kingfisher family and have a complex vocal repertoire. They use their vocalizations for various reasons, including territorial communication, establishing their presence within a group, and even to signal the time of day. These birds are known for their strong bonds with their family members, and they often engage in a communal "laughing" session where they vocalize together, reinforcing their social bonds. This behaviour is particularly common at dawn and dusk. The first time I heard a kookaburra was at dusk. I was all alone, threatened by this loud, unusual laughter. I wondered what animal had unleashed itself in the suburbs.

Since then, I have become quite accustomed to these beautiful birds. During my daily sauntering, I sometimes sit on the bench in the thickest of lush vegetation bush, watch the kookaburras, and listen to them. Watching their strong family bonds beckon and how the season change impacts their behaviour is fascinating. Nature demonstrates so much to us. These birds are famous for their robust family bonds and social behaviour, which is often demonstrated in various ways:

Cooperative breeding: Kookaburras are cooperative breeders, which means that multiple family members, often the previous year's offspring, assist the parents in raising the new chicks. This behaviour is commonly observed in many bird species and helps increase the chances of survival for the young.

Nesting and territory defense: Kookaburras are territorial birds, and family groups will defend their nesting territories together. Both parents and the older siblings work together to protect the nest from threats, such as predators or other intruding kookaburras.

Hunting and feeding together: Kookaburras are predatory birds and mainly feed on insects, small mammals, lizards, and even other birds. Family members often hunt and feed together, cooperating in capturing and sharing food resources, strengthening their bond.

Vocal communication: Kookaburras are highly vocal birds and use a variety of calls to communicate with each other. They have specific calls to strengthen the family bond and maintain social cohesion.

Roosting in groups: Kookaburras often roost together as a family, especially during the non-breeding season. This communal roosting behaviour fosters a sense of security and promotes social interaction within the family.

Learning and play: Young kookaburras learn essential life skills from their parents and older siblings. They engage in playful activities, such as mock hunting and aerial acrobatics, which help them develop necessary hunting skills and contribute to the bonding process.

Long-lasting partnerships: Kookaburras are known for forming long-lasting partnerships. Once they find a mate, they tend to stay together for several years, raising multiple broods together and further strengthening their family bonds.

Overall, the cooperative nature and social interactions of kookaburras contribute to establishing and maintaining strong family bonds, helping to ensure the survival and success of the entire family unit. Nature models family cohesiveness in a tangible way for us all to glean. Coping with the aftermath of a loved one's suicide can be an incredibly challenging and a painful experience. It is essential to recognize that grief is a natural process, and that healing takes time. When a family is in mourning, it is a telling tale of how the engineering of the family dynamics operates. Mourning refers to expressing grief, sorrow, and sadness over the loss of someone or something significant. It is a natural and universal human response to death, the end of a relationship, or any other profoundly impactful loss. During mourning, individuals may experience various emotions, such as sadness, anger, confusion, and loneliness.

Mourning is a culturally and socially influenced practice, and different societies have various customs and rituals. These customs may include wearing specific clothing, holding memorial services, conducting religious or spiritual ceremonies, or observing specific mourning periods. The purpose of mourning is to provide a framework for individuals to cope with their emotions, come to terms with the loss, and eventually find ways to move forward with their lives. It allows people to acknowledge the significance of what has been lost and to honour the memory of the deceased or the lost relationship. The mourning process is unique to each person and may take varying amounts of time, depending on the individual and the nature of the loss. Overall, mourning is an essential part of the human experience and can be a step towards healing and finding meaning in life after a significant loss.

During our mourning process, we witnessed robust bonds and unions with personal agendas. My brother was pushed to suicide due to prolonged malpractice, and those who were guilty now found new zeal to unleash another dose of venom rather than be cognisant of all the wounded hearts and the fact that an innocent person ended his life, rather than coming to the table with answers and leaving no stone unturned. The guilty made every effort to hide their tracks. Then, there was an undercurrent who had no concept of living the kookaburra lifestyle. The abundance of every heart rose to the surface, and we all got to see the contents of each heart. Some people do not just strike a nerve; they corrode every moral boundary, indulging in plausible deniability. I am at peace because I know I have kept it real, and I am not on earth to acquire but to make a difference in life in some tangible way. Discipline will take you to places where motivation cannot. I know without a shadow of a doubt that I made a palatable difference in Jayandra's life, which was reflected in my last conversation with him.

Mourning a suicidal death can be an incredibly complex and challenging experience, both for the immediate family and loved ones of the deceased, as well as for the wider community affected by the loss. The impact of such a loss can be profound and far-reaching, with emotional, psychological, and social consequences. Trauma comes from the horrid things that happened to us. It also stems from the loving things that did not happen to us. Here are some of the key impacts that may be experienced:

Intense grief and emotions: Losing someone to suicide can trigger intense and complicated emotions, including shock, disbelief, guilt, anger, sadness, and profound sorrow. The sudden and unexpected nature of suicide can make the grieving process even more difficult.

Stigma and isolation: Societal stigma surrounding suicide can exacerbate the grieving process. Some individuals may feel ashamed or reluctant to talk about the cause of death, leading to a sense of isolation and loneliness. Although grief can make you feel isolated, try to stay connected with others. Isolation can intensify feelings of sadness and despair.

Questions and "why?": Survivors of suicide loss may grapple with numerous questions, seeking to understand why their loved one took their life. The lack of clear answers can be frustrating and lead to prolonged distress.

Trauma and PTSD: Witnessing or finding the aftermath of a suicide can be traumatic for those directly involved, potentially leading to post-traumatic stress disorder (PTSD) symptoms. The PTSD is a mental health condition that can occur in individuals who have experienced or witnessed a traumatic event. The symptoms of PTSD can vary in intensity and duration and can affect different aspects of a person's life. Here are some common symptoms of PTSD:

- Intrusive thoughts: Recurrent, distressing memories of the traumatic event can also include nightmares or flashbacks, where the person feels as if they are reliving the traumatic experience.

- Avoidance: Individuals with PTSD may actively avoid anything that reminds them of the trauma. This could include avoiding certain places, people, activities, or even conversations related to the event.

- Adverse changes in thoughts and mood: This may involve feeling emotionally numb, experiencing persistent negative emotions (e.g., guilt, fear, anger), and losing interest in previously enjoyed activities. People with PTSD may also have difficulty remembering aspects of the traumatic event.

- Hyperarousal: Individuals may be constantly on edge, easily startled, and have difficulty sleeping. They may exhibit hypervigilance and have trouble concentrating.

- Changes in reactivity: Individuals with PTSD may experience increased irritability, aggression, or reckless behaviour. They might have difficulty managing their emotions and have frequent outbursts.

- Physical symptoms: These can include headaches, stomach aches, and other physical complaints that may not have a clear medical explanation.

It is important to note that not everyone who experiences a traumatic event will develop PTSD, and the severity of symptoms can vary from person to person. If you or someone you know is experiencing symptoms of PTSD, it is essential to seek help from a mental health professional. PTSD can be effectively treated through various therapies, such as cognitive-behavioural therapy (CBT), eye movement desensitization and reprocessing (EMDR), and medications, if necessary. Early intervention and support can significantly improve the prognosis and quality of life for individuals with PTSD.

Guilt and self-blame: Loved ones may experience guilt and self-blame, wondering if they could have done something differently to prevent suicide. These feelings are often unfounded but can be challenging to overcome.

Increased risk of suicide in survivors: Survivors of suicide loss, especially close family members, may face a higher risk of experiencing suicidal thoughts or behaviours themselves. It is crucial to seek support and professional help to address these risks.

Disrupted grief process: Mourning a suicide death can disrupt the typical grieving process, making it harder to find closure and acceptance. Accepting death while acknowledging the complexities of suicide can be particularly challenging.

Impact on relationships: Suicide loss can strain relationships within families and communities. People may react differently to grief, leading to misunderstandings or conflicts.

Mental health challenges: The grief and trauma resulting from a suicide death can contribute to or exacerbate mental health issues, such as depression and anxiety, in those affected.

Educational and occupational impacts: Grieving individuals may struggle to concentrate on work or studies, potentially impacting their performance and productivity.

Support and coping: It is crucial for those mourning a suicide death to have access to appropriate support and coping mechanisms. Professional counselling, support groups, and open communication can help navigate the grieving process.

Preventing future suicides: The loss of a loved one to suicide can motivate survivors to advocate for mental health awareness and suicide prevention, aiming to help others who may be struggling.

Seek support: Reach out to friends, family members, or a support group for those who have lost someone to suicide. Talking with others who have experienced similar losses can be comforting and validating.

Professional help: Consider speaking with a mental health professional or counsellor. They can provide guidance and support in processing your emotions and navigating through grief.

Allow yourself to grieve: Grieving is a natural and necessary process. Allow yourself to feel and express your emotions without judgment. There is no right or wrong way to grieve.

Self-care: Take care of yourself physically and emotionally. Ensure you eat well, get enough rest, and engage in activities that bring you comfort and joy.

Honour your loved one's memory: Consider finding ways to honour your brother's memory, such as by creating a tribute or participating in activities he enjoyed.

Be patient with yourself: Healing from the loss of a loved one takes time. Be patient and compassionate with yourself as you go through this process.

Limit exposure to media: Media coverage of suicide can be triggering. Try to limit your exposure to news or social media that may cause additional distress.

Seek closure: If possible, seek closure through any unanswered questions or unresolved issues. This might involve talking to friends or family or seeking support from a counsellor.

Avoid making major decisions: Grief can cloud judgment, so avoid making significant life decisions immediately after the loss.

Seek justice: Seeking justice for a suicide death can be a challenging and emotionally taxing process. It is important to remember that the legal and justice systems may vary depending on the country and jurisdiction involved. Here are some general steps you might consider taking:

- Contact authorities: Notify the police or relevant authorities immediately after the suicide death. They will investigate to determine the circumstances surrounding the death.

- Autopsy and investigation: A thorough investigation, including an autopsy, will be conducted to understand the cause of death and any potential contributing factors.

- Legal advice: Consult a lawyer specializing in wrongful death or civil litigation to explore your legal options. They can guide you through the legal process and advise you on the best action.

- File a civil lawsuit: Depending on the circumstances surrounding the suicide, you may consider filing a civil lawsuit against parties you believe contributed to the death. This could include healthcare providers, institutions, or individuals who may have been negligent in their duty of care.

- Management of the deceased estate and will: Ensure standard operating processes and protocols are followed. Challenge those who indulge in malpractice.

Remember that seeking justice for a suicide death can be a complex and lengthy process. Be prepared for challenges and remember to take care of yourself during this difficult time.

Pray for the soul: Praying for the soul of someone who has died by suicide can be a profoundly emotional and spiritual process. Here are some general guidelines on how you might approach this prayer:

- Create a Peaceful Environment: Find a quiet, peaceful space to focus and connect with your emotions and thoughts.

- Honesty and Vulnerability: Be open and honest with your feelings. Praying for the soul of someone who took their own life can be challenging, and it is okay to acknowledge the mix of emotions you may be experiencing, such as grief, sadness, confusion, or anger.

- Address the Deceased: You can begin the prayer by directly addressing the soul of the deceased person. You might use their name or say, "Dear [Name], may your soul find peace."

- Express Love and Compassion: Express your love and compassion for the deceased. Share positive memories of them and acknowledge their struggles and pain without judgment.

- Ask for Forgiveness: If you feel there were missed opportunities to offer support or if you have any feelings of guilt, ask for forgiveness. It is essential to remember that complex factors often influence suicidal thoughts and actions beyond any one individual's control.

- Pray for Peace and Healing: Pray for the person's soul to find peace and rest. You can also pray for comfort and healing for the family and friends grieving the loss.

- Seek Divine Mercy: Depending on your spiritual beliefs, you may ask for God's mercy and understanding in judging the person's actions.

- Support for Those Left Behind: Pray for support, strength, and healing for the loved ones who are mourning the loss of their dear ones.

- Seek Guidance for Yourself: Ask for guidance and wisdom as you grapple with the aftermath of the loss and strive to understand it better.

- Pray Regularly: You can incorporate praying for the deceased soul into your daily or weekly prayers. This ongoing practice can be comforting and help in the healing process.

Remember that each person's spiritual beliefs are unique, so feel free to adjust the prayer to align with your faith and understanding. Additionally, it might be helpful to seek support from religious or spiritual leaders, counsellors, or support groups as you navigate the complexities of grieving a suicide loss. It is important to recognise that mourning a suicide death is a highly individual experience, and people may react differently based on their personal history, cultural background, and support systems. Encouraging open dialogue, reducing stigma, and providing mental health resources are essential steps in helping those affected by suicide loss cope with their grief and move towards healing.

Remember, it is okay to ask for help when you need it. If you struggle to cope with the loss, do not hesitate to seek professional assistance. It is essential to have support as you work through your grief and healing process.

It was a hard pill for Jayandra to swallow, realising he meant nothing to the people that meant so much to him. Ensure everyone in your boat is rowing and not drilling holes when you are not looking—know your circle. Ensure people's actions align with their words. You will only have limited time on earth; today is an excellent start to doing something terrific. The strongest people are not those who show strength in front of us but fight battles that we know nothing about. No one stays with you permanently; learn to survive alone.

Most of us are not defeated in one decisive battle. We are defeated by one tiny, seemingly insignificant surrender at a time that chips away at the essence of who we are. God is still writing your story. Quit trying to steal the pen, trust the author. The suicide revolution is now. Do you have a genuine posture of compassion? The most prominent choice you can make to influence this landscape is to be a good person.

We can easily forgive a child who is afraid of the dark. The real tragedy of life is when men fear the light. If you know that God is with you in your journey through life, it does not matter who is against you. Bruce Lee said, **"Do not speak negatively about yourself as a joke; your body does not know the difference."** Words are energy, and they cast spells, enhance the way you speak about yourself, and you can change your life. You are not changing; you are choosing. Some are not healed by an apology. I read this post by the infamous Jay Shetty: **"My mum said stop being the go-to person for someone you cannot go to, and I felt that."** That sounds like great motherly advice. However, a comment caught my eye that read, **"Very false. Spreading your light has nothing to do with what you get in return. Bad advice!"**

Image 8: Tips to help you with anxiety.

A story from a fellow author about the entanglement of PTSD and the loss of her dad shared with permission:

Tribute to my father.

My father, through my eyes, was a great dad, a noble man, who suffered the aftermath as a returned veteran from World War Two.

One thunderous night, my father was found dead by a neighbour in the morning. He died from a bullet wound to his head from his own gun.

A life lost to PTSD was way too early.

PTSD or post-traumatic stress disorder is a silent killer that so many people suffer from. It is not the answer for someone with my father's talents and stature to succumb to. Yet, he suffered silently all those years, simmering with wrath underneath his exterior. His demeanour, like all returning soldiers, never showed visible signs of pain, nor did he speak about the war years or how he felt.

However, my mother knew that her young husband, who left his bride to go to war, was not the same man who returned to her, and his bursts of anger were directed at her all too often.

Sadly, she was a battered woman.

Mother never left Dad until her dying day, and Dad was grateful for her love, loyalty, and affection for him.

Dad was a high achiever. He was the school captain, the sports captain, and a popular guy around school.

My father was an attractive man, and he met my mother when he had acute appendicitis in the hospital. And she was his nurse, and so their love affair began.

They married in 1940, and he was given a week off from the Army to do this before he was commissioned to travel with his regiment to the Middle East.

Our father was always in control of our family affairs and looked after mum and us, three children, as well as he could, providing a good home, upbringing, and private schooling for which my siblings and I are very grateful.

My mother died after a prolonged battle with cancer, and it was after her death that Dad did not want to live anymore.

Dad was silent about his thoughts, and the first sign was when he attempted to commit suicide after our mother's death.

Suicide had not worked this time around when he took a bottle of sleeping tablets and drank it down with whiskey, falling onto the floor, foaming. It was one of his neighbours who found him and called the ambulance.

The hospital saved his life this time by pumping out the poison from his stomach, changing his blood, and then giving him a transfusion.

This shock must have been an ordeal for my dad. He was very apologetic about his actions, and we thought he was okay.

Dad came to visit me in Sydney during his holidays for my son's christening. It was such a joyful experience to have him here with us, his

two sisters, and their families.
I remember feeling so proud, waving to my father when he boarded that flight back to Perth, looking perfectly normal in his well-tailored grey suit. I did not know that time would be the last time I would see him alive.

After Dad returned to Perth, where he tragically took his own life with a single bullet, he was 62 years old and left us three adult children wondering why, so many questions and no answers.

Why so suddenly, why without a warning, and why when he was not physically ill? What did not we know about his emotional health—that he was mentally ill and exhausted from living without Mum?

My father had everything going for him, and he was physically healthy. He groomed himself well and diligently went to work every day, and we all loved him dearly.

Did Dad know this enough to keep him safe?

We do not have the answers for PTSD.
Our family was never the same after this tragic loss.

I salute my father for being a man of courage and for having attempted to hold high-profile jobs.

Father was one who always wanted to do good, who worked hard but could not hold down the job for long, which is a trait of PTSD.

Today, we are more aware of emotional wellness than 40 years ago, and so PTSD subtly allowed my father to take his own life. True, his life took a toll from the effects of serving his country, but war sadly could not save him from himself.

My name is Helen Ena Glen, and I live in Sydney, Australia, with my husband and children around me.

I am proud to be the eldest daughter of Noel and Ena.

My brother David and his wife were invited to have dinner with Dad, and he was happy to have them over and cook a simple meal himself. When they left, they suggested a good movie for Dad to watch.

The night was thunderous, and so it was during the storms that tragic night that Dad took his life.

It was a dreadful shock for my brother to be informed by the police of the situation and about the circumstances of the loss.

Dreadful.

My sister was eight months pregnant and could not fly to Perth for Dad's funeral, but her life was ruined by the news of her father's passing away *so tragically.*

We often talk about our love, deep respect, and gratitude for our parents, the life they provided us, and the happier times.

Life goes on, and we show a brave face through unending tears, but we must be thankful for the family support and love shown towards us during the time of losing our beloved father and loved one. It is good to always ask, "Are you okay?" if you know things are not all that well with someone, these three words can save a life.

Helen Glen

You are not yourself when you are triggered. You become who you think you ought to be to survive. When you are constantly triggered, your identity can start to slip away. Your personality and values are constantly hijacked by fight or flight reflexes. Here are some tips to control your thoughts and guidance to control your self-talk:

~~Why didn't I start earlier?~~

The past cannot be changed. There is no better time to start than now.

~~What is the point of making an effort, tomorrow is not guaranteed.~~

I will treat each day as the last and make the most of it.

~~This is too difficult. I cannot do it.~~

Success comes with a lot of hardships; perseverance is the key.

~~I have to start from scratch while others are born with an advantage.~~

Everyone has a different journey and comparing will waste your energy. Channel your energy positively.

Although my brother's suicide had a profound effect on my life, I did not permit it to ruin me. I burned incense and prayed for his soul to rest in peace. I forgave Jayandra for his choice. I beseeched him to forgive me for my shortfall in not recognising his plight. The pungent smell of cheeky chutney floods my memory glands and taste buds – Jayandra's favourite, and he was a master chef at conjuring this up. The toasty, warm smell of him cooking dinner for his dog, Whiskey, will always warm my heart. The jingle jangle of his fishing bag is a sound that I will always savour. Watching him drop sea sand all over the freshly cleaned house are some of my favourite things. The swish of his fishing rod and watching him cast a line and reel in the biggest fish in the country with a disabled hand will forever be etched in my heart and cherished. I can close my eyes and take myself to any of the above memories in a flash.

Jayandra, the fabric of your existence is embedded in our lives and will always be. This book forms part of your rich legacy. Always remember that the people who are candy to your eyes can poison your heart. Study their ingredients before feeding your soul. Never try to squeeze sympathy and support from a rag that has been dry since birth. Some burdens are so heavy. However, God allows us to testify to certain dexterity to put down the heaviest of them: anger, resentment, pride, and ego. Even though death has swept through our home, we will not allow the conviction to sting our lives; the scorpions of the world will sting themselves. Many years ago, Mark Twain said, **"It is curious that physical courage should be so common in the world and moral courage so rare."** Have you ever challenged yourself to grow moral courage?

"Never judge the future of a person from the present conditions; time has the power to change a black hole into a shining diamond." - unknown.

Jayandra's Cheeky Chutney Recipe

Ingredients:

- Six ripe tomatoes roasted in open flames or grilled in an oven
- Four green chillies, finely chopped
- One red onion, finely chopped
- Six cloves of garlic
- Three sprigs of spring onions with the bulbs finely chopped
- ¼ cup of coriander, finely chopped
- ¼ cup of mint leaves, finely chopped
- Freshly ground black pepper
- One lemon, freshly squeezed
- Salt to taste

Method:

Peel off the skin from the roasted tomatoes and blend with the garlic thoroughly in an electric blender for 10-15 minutes. Add the remaining chopped ingredients and mix well. Refrigerate. Add salt, pepper, and lemon juice just before serving.

Serving suggestion:

- A condiment to a meal
- On pappadum's
- On bruschetta
- In a roti roll
- An addition to dosa filling
- On cheese toast
- Mixed in with chakalaka
- A side dish to bunny chow
- Topping on grilled sourdough bread
- Served with pap and boerewors
- Supplement to wrap filling

- Add-on in tacos
- Inclusion to any sandwich

May you create exceptional memories with this simple culinary delight from Jayandra.

9. Concepts to Transform Your Life

Phillip Island in Australia is known for its remarkable penguin conservation success story. The island, located in Victoria, is famous for its large population of little penguins, also known as fairy penguins, the smallest species of penguins in the world. Conservation efforts on Phillip Island have been ongoing for several decades, focusing on protecting and preserving the penguin colonies that inhabit the island's coastline. Here are some key aspects of the penguin conservation success story on Phillip Island:

Penguin parade: The main attraction for tourists on Phillip Island is the *"Penguin Parade,"* where visitors can watch the penguins return to their burrows after a day of fishing at sea. This event is well-managed and regulated to minimize disturbance to the penguins while offering a unique opportunity for people to observe these charming creatures in their natural habitat.

Wildlife reserves: The Phillip Island Nature Parks organization manages several protected wildlife reserves, including the penguin colonies and their surrounding habitat. These reserves are crucial for providing safe breeding grounds and protecting the penguins from predators and human disturbances.

Boardwalks and viewing platforms: Specially designed boardwalks and viewing platforms have been constructed to allow visitors to observe the penguins without causing harm to their nesting areas. These structures ensure a positive experience for both tourists and penguins alike.

Research and monitoring: Ongoing research and monitoring programs help track the penguin populations and better understand their behaviour, feeding patterns, and breeding habits. This data is vital for making informed conservation decisions.

Public education: Local authorities and conservation organizations conduct educational programs and awareness campaigns to inform the public about the importance of protecting penguins and their fragile coastal habitat.

Environmental stewardship: Phillip Island's community and local businesses actively participate in conservation efforts, promoting sustainable practices and minimizing their environmental impact to safeguard the penguins' future.

Thanks to these collective efforts, the little penguin population on Phillip Island has thrived, and the conservation success story has inspired other wildlife preservation initiatives worldwide. We can take a leaf out of this book of success; where there is a will, there is a way. I desire to one day have a success story for the prevention of suicide. We can all work in concert with each other to achieve this.

Suicide is the act of killing oneself on purpose. The complexity that unravels in many layers may mean various things to different people: catastrophe, heartbreak, disbelief, dread, rage, misery, relief, shame, stigma, a broken legacy, a cry for help, release from pain, selfishness, heroic, at peace, the final say, punishment, revenge, trauma, unloved, no way out, and cop out. Every precious life is so much more than these mere adjectives. It is a person who is sincerely loved. It does not seem to matter what part of your back you are stabbed in. The blade always reaches the heart! Sometimes, it is tough to move on, but once you move to a better space, you will realise it is the best decision you have ever made. Sometimes, there is no support system. It is just you and the universe; this is your vision and life, so get laser focused. Here are some Japanese concepts to transform your life:

Ikigai: Discover your purpose in life. Determine the reason you wake up each morning. Choose something that aligns with your strengths, passions, and the world's needs. This is what gives life meaning.

Shikita ga nai: Let go of what you cannot change. Recognise that some things are just out of your control, and that is okay. Let go and focus on what you can change.

Wabi-sadi: Find peace in imperfection. Recognise that nothing in life is perfect, including yourself and others. Instead of striving for flawlessness, find joy in the imperfections that make life unique.

Gaman: Preserve your dignity during tough times. Show emotional maturity and self-control, even when faced with challenges. Remember to be patient, resilient, and understanding.

Obaitori: Do not compare yourself to others. Everyone has a different timeline and a unique part. It is important to focus on your progress rather than trying to measure yourself against others.

Kaizen: Always seek to improve in all areas of your life. Even small changes can add up and make a significant impact over time.

Shu-Ha-Ri: *"When the student is ready, the teacher will appear. When the student is truly ready, the teacher will disappear."* - Tao Te Ching.

It is a way of thinking about how to learn and master techniques. There are three stages to acquiring knowledge:

- ♦ Shu: Learn the basics by following the teachings of one master.
- ♦ Ha: Start experimenting, learn from masters, and integrate the learning into practice.

- Ri: Focus on innovation and the ability to apply your learning to various situations.

The most important spiritual growth does not happen when meditating on a yoga mat. It happens during conflict when you are frustrated, angry, or scared, and you are doing the same old thing and suddenly realise that you have a choice to do it differently.

Suicidology is the scientific study of suicide, suicidal behaviour, and suicide prevention. It is a multidisciplinary field that brings together experts from various disciplines, such as psychology, psychiatry, sociology, public health, medicine, and epidemiology, to understand the complex factors and causes that contribute to suicidal thoughts and actions. Suicidology aims to improve our knowledge of suicide risk factors, protective factors, and the underlying mechanisms that lead individuals to contemplate or attempt suicide. By studying suicide from different angles and perspectives, researchers and professionals in this field strive to develop effective prevention strategies and interventions to reduce suicide rates and support those at risk. It is essential to note that suicidology does not focus solely on preventing suicide after it becomes an immediate concern. Instead, it aims to understand the broader factors at play and how to address them proactively to prevent suicidal behaviours from occurring in the first place. Suicide prevention is a crucial aspect of suicidology, but the field encompasses much more, including postvention (support for those affected by suicide) and ongoing research to refine prevention efforts.

Revulsion has stolen a narrative with force for far too long. Insatiability has so intensely robbed you. Lies have embezzled you for a prolonged time. It is now a new season for you. Let love stop muttering and leap into change. Transform to create a new lease on your life. Here are five ways to inspire yourself daily:

- Listen to something or someone inspirational for 15-30 minutes daily.
- Speak positively to yourself about yourself. Never be your own worst critic. Be your best encourager.
- Read or listen to a book that inspires you for 15-30 minutes daily. The bible is my go-to for an inspirational non-fiction book.
- Act on the things that align with your purpose and values every day.
- Do your best to shun distractions and lead your life with intention.

When prioritising these daily habits, you will never lack inspiration and motivation. Your purpose will default to alignment.

The Theory of Change (TOC) is a systematic approach used by

organizations, initiatives, or projects to define their long-term goals and map out the necessary steps to achieve those goals. It is a planning and evaluation framework that helps stakeholders understand the causal relationships between the actions taken, the outcomes expected, and the ultimate impact they seek to create. You can also use this approach in your personal life. A Theory of Change typically consists of the following components:

Vision and long-term goals: It begins with clearly articulating the desired outcomes or impacts the organization or project aims to achieve.

Impact pathways: The TOC outlines the sequence of outcomes and changes expected to occur towards the long-term goals. This involves identifying the intermediate outcomes, the short-term outcomes, and the relationships between them.

Assumptions: The TOC acknowledges the underlying assumptions about the interventions, external factors, and context influencing the expected outcomes. These assumptions need to be tested and validated during implementation.

Interventions and activities: It describes the specific interventions, strategies, and activities that will be implemented to bring about the intended outcomes.

Indicators and measures: The TOC identifies the key indicators that will be used to measure progress and success at each stage of the impact pathway.

Learning and adaptation: The TOC emphasizes continuous learning and adaptation throughout the implementation process. It encourages organizations to gather data and evidence to assess the effectiveness of their strategies and make necessary adjustments.

A Theory of Change aims to provide a clear roadmap for program planning, implementation, and evaluation. It helps stakeholders understand the logic behind the program's design and allows them to make informed decisions about resource allocation, monitor progress effectively, and improve their approaches based on evidence. By using a Theory of Change, organizations can enhance their accountability and transparency, increase the likelihood of achieving their goals, and demonstrate the effectiveness of their interventions.

I have adapted the TOC to a personalized approach. Reflect on these core components so you can write down where you are and where you would like to be. Remember that you may need to take baby steps. It is okay to begin with small actions in the right direction. Your valiant effort here is to start the change process.

Theory of Change	What you know	Your strength comes from lifting yourself every time you were knocked out.
	When	Your goal is to grow so strong on the inside that nothing on the outside can affect your inner wellness without your conscious permission.
	Then	Be grateful for the many things in your life that bring you joy and comfort.
	How	Express deep appreciation for the small steps you achieve daily.
	Why	Choose to be kind to yourself and to love yourself unconditionally.
	Gratitude	Be grateful that every experience has created a better version of yourself.
	Always	Control your **ANGER** because it us just one letter away from **'D' ANGER**.

It is never too late to change your story and rebalance your scales. Make the call to no longer be a passenger, waiting for the universe to refund you a debt that was not owed, even if it is unsettled or stolen from you. Break patterns of codependency, overcome insomnia and low self-esteem. All these are lessons that will soothe your bleeding heart. Journaling is a great tool to whisper your thoughts and analyse your growth.

Prayer helps to balance your scales, especially when you have more questions than answers.

Create a safe healing altar. The prudent approach is to be proactive. No one is more responsible for your motivation than you. You must be intentional about taking steps to inspire yourself every day. Cultivating hope and reshaping perspectives are essential for personal growth and emotional well-being. Both practices can help us navigate difficult times, overcome challenges, and find meaning in our lives. Here are some strategies to cultivate hope and reshape perspectives:

Practice gratitude: Gratitude is a powerful tool for shifting perspective. Focus on the positive aspects of your life and express appreciation for them. Even during tough times, there are often small blessings to be thankful for, and recognizing them can help you see things in a more hopeful light.

Set realistic goals: Create attainable and meaningful goals for yourself. Having something to work towards can instill a sense of purpose and hope for the future. Break larger goals into smaller, manageable steps, and celebrate your achievements.

Learn from challenges: Instead of viewing challenges as roadblocks, see them as opportunities for growth and learning. Embrace the lessons they offer and use them to build resilience and strength.

Surround yourself with positive influences: Surround yourself with people who uplift and support you. Positive influences can inspire hope and offer different perspectives on your circumstances.

Practice mindfulness and meditation: Mindfulness helps you stay present in the moment and reduces anxiety about the future. Meditation can also help reshape negative thought patterns and foster a positive outlook.

Engage in activities you enjoy: Participate in activities that bring you joy and fulfilment. Engaging in hobbies and interests can provide a sense of purpose and positivity in daily life.

Seek support: Do not be afraid to seek support from friends, family, or a professional counsellor. Talking about your feelings and experiences can help you gain new perspectives and find hope in challenging situations.

Avoid dwelling on the past: While reflecting on past experiences can be helpful for growth, avoid dwelling on adverse events that you cannot change. Instead, focus on the present and what you can do to improve your future.

Practice self-compassion: Be kind to yourself and avoid self-criticism. Treat yourself with the same compassion and understanding you would offer a friend facing similar challenges.

Limit exposure to negativity: Be mindful of the media and information you consume. Limit exposure to negative news or social media content that can influence your perspective negatively.

Visualize a positive future: Take time each day to visualize a positive and hopeful future for yourself. Imagine the steps you need to take to get there and believe in your ability to achieve it.

Remember that cultivating hope and reshaping perspectives is an ongoing process that takes time and effort. Be patient with yourself and celebrate the progress you make along the way. Over time, these practices can have a transformative effect on your outlook and overall well-being. Nelson Mandela said: *"There is no passion to be found playing small; the greatest glory in living lies not in never failing but in rising every time we fail."* All moments or challenges we face in life are opportunities for:

- Growth in your thinking
- Elevation of your thoughts, beliefs, and programming
- Expansion into becoming the best version of yourself
- The development of your consciousness

A beautiful life with incredible moments awaits you on the other side of fear and doubt when you lead yourself with courage, conviction, and trust. Never allow fears or your subconscious programming to hold you back. You were born great. You have ample pluck to birth your vision, your life, and the reality you desire. When a storm comes into your life, it is erratic and bewildering. Your natural reaction is to contest it. However, sometimes, you need a disturbance in your repetition. As creatures of habit, we tend to stick to the same patterns and routines. Even when they no longer serve us. We are apt to continue doing them because they are familiar and safe. Instead of asking, "Why is this happening to me?" maybe you should ask, "What can I learn from this?" Not all storms come to disrupt your life, and some come to clear your path.

Living with a disabled hand has been a challenging journey, one that has required Jayandra to dig deep within himself to find hope and resilience. At times, it felt as though life had dealt him an unfair hand, quite literally. Simple tasks that most people take for granted had become monumental challenges. However, amidst the frustration and despair, he discovered an inner strength I never knew he possessed. Jayandra learned to adapt, finding new ways to accomplish daily tasks and pursuing his passions with unwavering determination. Each small triumph, whether mastering a new technique or gaining a greater sense of independence, became a beacon of hope in his life. His disabled hand may have limited him physically, but it has expanded his capacity for perseverance and appreciation for the resilience of the human spirit. Through this journey, I have understood that hope is not merely a fleeting emotion but a powerful force that can thrive even in the face of adversity, reminding me that life's challenges can catalyse profound personal growth.

Life throws us curve balls, the game changer is how we manage that challenge. I salute Jayandra for marching on with resilience and fortitude for more than three decades!

Image 9: A Salute to Jayandra

I watched Jayandra struggle to button his shirt when he was discharged from the hospital. I offered to help him. Our eyes met, and I felt something that I could not articulate. Sometimes, pain can be an enigma, an indescribable force that defies comprehension. It is a visceral, gnawing sensation that claws at the edges of consciousness, leaving one grappling in the depths of their vulnerability. This pain transcends words, making it nearly impossible to articulate or share with others. It is a solitary battle, a silent scream echoing within the confines of one's soul. In moments like these, all we can do is embrace the uncertainty, seek solace in the presence of loved ones, and hope that time will eventually soften the edges of this relentless agony, allowing us to grasp its meaning, even if it remains forever elusive. I watched him transcend to using his disabled hand like he did not even have a disability. Jayandra mastered the game of pool. He was second to none. He did not allow his disability to stop him. He buttoned his shirt and everything in between. Did the blow soften, or did he find a way to live despite the limitations?

"If you do not fill your day with high priority actions that inspire you, your day will be filled up with low priority distractions that don't." - Dr John Demartini.

10. What Good Can Spark?

My heart broke when I saw another tragic incident at the Shamwari Game Reserve in Eastern Cape Town, South Africa. Poaching and illegal hunting are indeed significant issues that pose a threat to many endangered species, including rhinos. The loss of a mother rhino is not only devastating for the staff at the reserve but also has long-term consequences for the survival of the species. It is important to understand that while some people may resort to poaching due to economic hardships and the struggle for survival, it is not a justifiable or a sustainable solution. Poaching and illegal hunting are illegal and unethical practices that harm wildlife populations, disrupt ecosystems, and threaten biodiversity. Addressing the root causes of poaching requires a multi-faceted approach, which includes:

Conservation efforts: Supporting and funding conservation organisations and initiatives that protect endangered species and their habitats can play a vital role in safeguarding wildlife.

Community involvement: Engaging with local communities living near wildlife reserves is essential. By creating alternative livelihoods and providing education and awareness about the importance of conservation, we can help reduce poaching incidents.

Law enforcement and penalties: Strengthening and rigorously enforcing laws to deter potential poachers and smugglers.

Global cooperation: Poaching is often driven by international demand for wildlife products. Collaborating at a global level to combat illegal wildlife trafficking is crucial.

Tourism: Responsible wildlife tourism can contribute positively to conservation efforts by providing economic incentives to local communities for protecting wildlife.

Technological advancements: Implementing surveillance technologies like drones, GPS tracking, and camera traps can help monitor and protect vulnerable wildlife populations.

Public awareness: Raising awareness about the consequences of poaching and the importance of wildlife conservation can garner public support and empathy for these issues.

It is essential to understand that while people may face challenges, resorting to illegal and harmful activities like poaching is not a solution. Long-term solutions must be pursued to address both human needs and wildlife conservation to ensure a balanced and harmonious coexistence between humans and the natural world. Always remember that you create the legacy that you leave behind. You cannot steal, stab someone in the heart, or indulge in malpractice yet be under the misconception that you lead a wholesome ethical life. Every action has a reaction, and your indiscretions affect humans in profound ways. Humans will never forget how you made them feel, regardless of what lip service you render.

Loyalty is not grey. It is black and white. You are either totally loyal or not loyal at all. And people have to understand this. You can only be loyal when it serves you. When you want to know your tribe, speak your truth, and see who sticks around. Be remembered for standing up for what is right when nobody else did, and if you do not know the whole story, keep your mouth shut. Be the game changer; the world has enough followers. You are not obligated to maintain a relationship with anyone who treats you poorly. If you have to tiptoe around others, you are not walking amongst your tribe. Authentic connection is born where toleration ends. Whatever you tolerate, you cannot change it. If you do not know the value of loyalty, you will never understand the damage of betrayal.

Never re-friend someone who has tried to destroy your character, money, or relationship. A snake only sheds its skin to become a bigger snake. Refrain from giving anyone the benefit of the doubt. People are what they show you. People who consistently and consciously hurt you do not deserve more chances. They deserve to be denied access. Establishing healthy boundaries is about having the courage to love yourself even when you risk disappointing others. People treat you exactly how they feel about you. Be blind if you want to be. Life is not about who you impress but about who you impact. Fake family and friends do not appreciate it when your authenticity is louder than their façade. Always take a stand for what is right. And if you end up standing alone, then frankly, stand-alone.

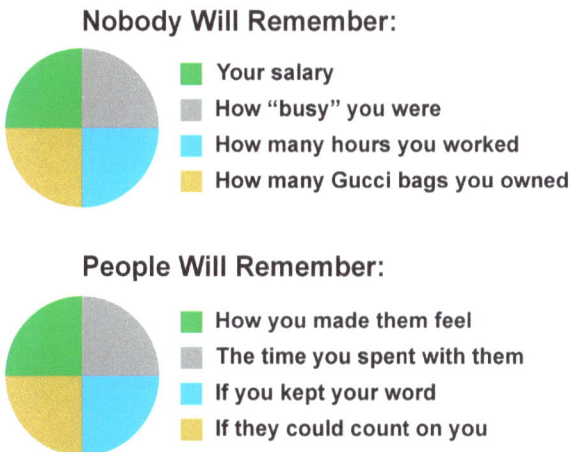

Image 10: What people will REMEMBER

You no longer fear the storms when you have learned how to be calm in the chaos. The ego says: I will find peace once everything falls into place. The spirit utters, find peace, and everything will fall into place. You will always have problems. Learn to enjoy life while solving them. There comes a point when you realise who matters, who never did, who will not anymore, and who always will. And in the end, you will learn who is fake, who is true, and who would risk it all for you. Never take constructive criticism from people who have not constructed anything. It would be best to stop asking people for directions to places they have never been. The reality is that one day, you will share your last moment with someone you love. Neither of you may know that it is your last moment. You will never realise that this was your last chance to say what you wanted to say or do what you wanted to do. You have a choice today to never live in regret and to learn to make every encounter meaningful.

Social media is not a book of life. It captures more good moments than bad; even the algorithms will help. Genuine connection happens in real-time, not screen time. When the alteration of life comes knocking, it will bring forth cycles of tangible and metaphoric death. Having an authentic connection with people who genuinely care for you makes all the difference in your world. Establish your network consciously. When you vibrate at a specific frequency, you not only hear it but also feel it. Your soul is always going to whisper the truth back to you. Your soul wants the best for you. And if you try to silence its voice, eventually, the whisper will become a roar. However, much you deny the truth, the truth goes on existing. Become more aware of what is worth your energy. How long will you let yourself be carried along by life as a passive participant? What will it take for you to stop and navigate your authentic path? Grow your knowledge of yourself so that it becomes a compass that leads you forward and will continue to lead you forward. Surround yourself with people who will fight for you in the rooms that you are absent in. Loyalty is not who is at your celebration table. Loyalty is standing next to you when you are at rock bottom. Who will answer your call when you are about to end your life?

The door to your heart should always be open. However, you must renovate the front porch so that humanity will have to step up to visit you now. ***"This above all: to thine own self be true, and it must follow, as the night the day, thou canst not then befalls any man. - William Shakespeare***. Shakespeare highlights that to maintain honest relations with others, we must first be true to ourselves. The illiterate in this era will not be those who cannot read and write but those who cannot learn, unlearn, and relearn. To learn, unlearn, and relearn is a concept that emphasizes the importance of adaptability and continuous growth in the process of acquiring knowledge and skills. It involves three interconnected stages:

Learn: This is the initial stage of acquiring new information, skills, or knowledge. Learning can happen through various means, such as formal education, training, reading, observation, and experiences. It is the foundation upon which you build your understanding of a subject or concept.

Unlearn: Unlearning is letting go of outdated, incorrect, or obsolete information or beliefs that may hinder your progress or limit your ability to learn new things effectively. It involves recognizing that some of the knowledge or practices you acquired may no longer be valid or useful in the current context. Unlearning requires openness to new perspectives and the willingness to challenge preconceived notions.

Relearn: After unlearning, relearning comes into play. Relearning involves updating your knowledge and skills based on new and relevant information. It allows you to adapt to changes in your environment, industry, or personal circumstances. Relearning builds upon your knowledge and helps you stay current and competitive in a rapidly evolving world.

The concepts of learn, unlearn, and relearn are often attributed to futurist and visionary Alvin Toffler. In a rapidly changing world where technology and knowledge evolve quickly, the ability to unlearn outdated ideas and relearn new ones becomes crucial for personal and professional development. Being open to continuous learning and adapting to change helps individuals and organizations thrive in dynamic environments.

No matter what yesterday was like, birds always start the new day with a song. You need to go to two places often: the place that heals you and the place that inspires you. Sometimes, people do not like you because you are not easily fooled. There are so many who can figure out the costs and so few who can discern the measure of value, the real value of an authentic relationship. You are permitted to be both a masterpiece and a work in progress simultaneously; know when to walk away while in certain phases of life. When your circle gets smaller, your vision will come into focus. There is strength and loyalty, not numbers. Never walk through life looking for evidence that you do not belong because you will always find it. Instead, always know the fact that you are worthy. The dead cannot speak; it is the living we need to watch. Do not treat people as bad as they are. Treat them as good as you are. Never forget that walking away from something unhealthy is brave. Understand deeply that what people do is never a reflection of you and is always their perception of life.

A few celebrities have vanished like morning dew:

1. Robin Williams, 1951-2014 - Robin Williams was an American comedian and actor.
2. Kurt Cobain, 1967-1994 - Kurt Cobain was an American musician and lead singer of Nirvana.
3. Marilyn Monroe, 1926-1962 - Marilyn Monroe was an American actress and model, considered an iconic figure of the 1950s.

Victims of suicide come from all walks of life, not just those who are perceived to be unfortunate. Suicidal thoughts are complex and can affect anyone, regardless of their fame or status. While celebrities may seem to have glamorous and successful lives, they are not immune to the same struggles and challenges that anyone else might face. It is important to remember that discussing individual cases of suicide can be harmful and invasive, as it can lead to sensationalising or glamorising the issue. Instead, it is essential to focus on the broader problem of human welfare and suicide prevention for everyone, regardless of their fame or status. Encouraging open conversations about mental health, reducing stigma, and providing access to mental health support are critical steps in addressing this serious issue. If you or someone you know is struggling with suicidal thoughts or mental health issues, please seek help from a mental health professional or a helpline in your country.

Never allow intermittent adversity to corrode your vision. Always look for brighter opportunities to colour in your life's canvas. The scripture is in the New Testament of the Bible, specifically the book of Romans. ***"And we know that in all things God works for the good of those who love him, who have been called according to his purpose." - Romans 8:28.***

This verse emphasizes the belief that God can bring good even out of challenging or difficult circumstances for those who have faith in and love Him. It offers comfort and reassurance to believers, knowing that God is ultimately in control and working things out for their benefit, according to His divine plan. Take courage that your situation will change, and a better season will emerge. Never give up. For those who are already grappling with the suicide of a loved one, as hard as it is, look for the silver lining. Rest assured that something good will spark from this vile experience. You may need to practice the logotherapy that we discussed earlier to shift the focus to helping others. Perhaps start a reform for suicide prevention. Find what works for you. A lesson always accompanies the experience.

Breaking someone's trust is like crumpling up a perfect piece of paper. You can smooth it over, but it will never be the same. Discern how to control the circle that influences you. Detachment does not mean hatred. It means you no longer align or allow negative energy to derail you. Realise that your behaviour may affect another person adversely. Here are some psychological hacks that will help you control a situation:

- ♦ When someone answers your question partially, wait. Do not interrupt. Chances are, they will complete the answer when you say nothing.

- ♦ When you need something from someone, frame it as an offer or opportunity instead of a request.

- ♦ When you meet people, notice their eye colour while you smile at them. Do not mention anything about it. It is a good way to ensure you make a real connection with them.

- A person's name is the sweetest sound in the world to that person. To make a person feel very special, I remember and repeat their name.

- I have zero expectations when I first try something new; it prevents disappointment.

- To change a person's character, not just how they treat people, bless someone who cannot do anything for you.

- After you state your position in a negotiation, wait for a while. If you continue to speak, you are not speaking in your favour.

- Chewing gum while doing nerve-wracking things can calm your brain.

- When you are learning something, teach someone about it. You will remember it easily and explore more in the process of teaching.

- Most people's favourite subject is to talk about themselves. Ask simple questions if you do not know what to talk about or have an awkward silence.

- Emotional expression causes emotion. When you force yourself to smile, your mood will improve.

- Stand up straight. It makes you look more confident, and you will feel more confident.

- With kids, frame things so that I always give them a choice. It makes them feel like they are in control. For example, "Do you want to wear a red or blue shirt?" Either way, they know it is time to put on a shirt.

Unbelonging, a sense of not fitting in or feeling disconnected from others and one's environment, can significantly affect a person's well-being and overall life experience. Here are some ways in which unbelonging can impact an individual:

Emotional distress: Feeling like you do not belong can lead to feelings of loneliness, sadness, and anxiety. It can create a sense of isolation and emotional pain, making it challenging to form meaningful connections with others.

Low self-esteem: When a person feels like they do not belong, they may start questioning their self-worth and value. This can lead to low self-esteem and self-doubt, affecting their confidence and ability to engage in social interactions.

Social withdrawal: The feeling of not belonging might lead to a desire to withdraw from social situations. This can perpetuate a cycle of isolation, as avoiding social interactions can further reinforce the belief that one does not fit in.

Identity issues: Unbelonging can lead to confusion about one's identity and place in the world. It can create a struggle to understand who they are and where they belong, potentially leading to a search for identity and purpose.

Mental health challenges: Persistent feelings of unbelonging can contribute to mental health issues such as depression, anxiety, and even more severe conditions if left unaddressed.

Academic or professional challenges: In academic or work settings, feeling like an outsider may affect a person's performance and willingness to engage actively. This can hinder opportunities for learning, growth, and advancement.

Physical health impact: Long-term stress resulting from a sense of unbelonging can take a toll on a person's physical health, contributing to issues like headaches, insomnia, and a weakened immune system.

Coping mechanisms: Some individuals may develop harmful coping mechanisms like substance abuse or engaging in risky behaviours to escape the pain of not belonging.

It is important to note that the impact of unbelonging can vary from person to person, and some individuals may be more resilient in handling these feelings. Additionally, situations and circumstances may change, allowing individuals to find a sense of belonging in different environments or through new relationships. Addressing feelings of unbelonging often involves seeking support from friends, family, or professionals. Therapy and counselling can help explore these emotions and develop strategies to improve social connections and self-acceptance. Building connections with like-minded individuals or engaging in activities that align with personal interests can also help foster a sense of belonging and acceptance. What good can you spark with those who are in your network? Do you make people feel like they belong?

"If your actions create a legacy that inspires others to dream more, learn more, do more, and become more, then you are an excellent leader." - Dolly Parton.

11. Grief and Trauma

Suicide certainly has no rational logic. If I could determine that X is a result of Y, then I would have been able to formulate a plan Z to remedy the pain. Sadly, there are no formulae. We are all blessed with life. However, each person's terrain, struggle, opportunities, difficulties, trials, and triumphs differ. Whatever we face, we have a choice: we will be hindered by hurdles or advance through perseverance. Like oxygen to a fire, obstacles become fuel for the blaze that fans ambition; this can also be your choice. Whatever end of the spectrum you are stuck at, victim of suicide death or contemplating suicide, the options are all around you. The obstacle in your way will become your path. Never forget that every obstacle is an opportunity to mend your situation. What has got you stuck?

Trauma is a heavy burden to bear. It can cast a long shadow over our lives, affecting our thoughts, emotions, and behaviours. But the human spirit is remarkably resilient, and the journey to healing and transcendence is worth exploring. In this chapter, I will delve into the process of transcending trauma, offering insights and guidance to help you move from pain to resilience. Trauma and grief are two distinct psychological experiences, although they can sometimes overlap or coexist in certain situations. Here is a breakdown of the key differences between trauma and grief:

Trauma:

Definition: Trauma refers to an emotional response to a distressing or deeply disturbing event or series of events that overwhelms an individual's ability to cope. It is often characterised by feelings of extreme fear, helplessness, or horror.

Causes: Traumatic events can vary widely, such as natural disasters, accidents, violence, abuse, war, or witnessing a traumatic event happening to others.

Symptoms: Trauma can lead to a range of emotional, psychological, and physical symptoms. These may include flashbacks, nightmares, hypervigilance, avoidance of reminders, emotional numbness, difficulty concentrating, irritability, insomnia, and a sense of detachment.

Treatment: Trauma can be addressed through various therapeutic approaches, such as trauma-focused therapy, cognitive-behavioural therapy (CBT), eye movement desensitization and reprocessing (EMDR), and medication in some cases.

Eye Movement Desensitization and Reprocessing (EMDR) is a

psychotherapy approach used to help individuals deal with distressing or traumatic memories. It was initially developed to treat post-traumatic stress disorder (PTSD) but has been applied to various other mental health issues. During EMDR therapy, the person is asked to recall distressing memories while focusing on external stimuli, typically guided by the therapist's finger movements, lights, or sounds. This bilateral stimulation is thought to help the individual process and reprocess the traumatic memory, reducing its emotional impact. The exact mechanisms of how EMDR works are still a subject of research and debate, but many people have reported benefits from this therapy in terms of reducing the emotional distress associated with traumatic experiences. It is important to seek EMDR therapy from a qualified and trained therapist if you are considering it as a treatment option.

Grief:

Definition: Grief is a natural response to a significant loss or bereavement, typically associated with the death of a loved one. It involves a complex emotional, cognitive, and behavioural adjustment process to cope with the loss.

Causes: Grief primarily arises from the death of someone close, but it can also result from other significant losses like the end of a relationship, the loss of a job, or the diagnosis of a terminal illness.

Symptoms: Grief manifests differently for individuals, but common symptoms include intense sadness, longing for the deceased, shock, disbelief, guilt, anger, difficulty accepting the loss, changes in appetite or sleep patterns, and difficulty concentrating or functioning.

Treatment: Grief is often addressed through supportive therapies, such as grief counselling, support groups, and interventions that help individuals navigate the grieving process. There is no fixed timeline for grief, as it is a highly individual and personal experience.

While grief is typically a response to loss, trauma can result from a wide range of distressing events beyond loss. Both trauma and grief can have significant impacts on an individual's emotional well-being and may require professional support and intervention to promote healing and recovery. When someone dies by suicide, the effects on those left behind can be profound and complex. What people remember after a suicide varies greatly, depending on their relationship with the individual and the circumstances surrounding the death. Here are some common aspects that people may remember:

Emotional impact: The pain and shock of losing someone to suicide can be overwhelming. Loved ones may remember the intense emotions they experienced upon hearing the news and grappling with the realization that the person they cared about was no longer with them.

Struggles and challenges: People may remember the difficulties the individual faced in their life, such as mental health issues, personal problems, or external stressors that may have contributed to their decision to end their life.

Guilt and regret: Those close to the person who died by suicide might remember feeling guilty or regretful for not recognizing the signs or for being unable to prevent the tragedy. They may wonder if there was more they could have done.

Unanswered questions: Suicide often leaves people with many unanswered questions. Friends and family might try to understand why the person chose to end their life, but sometimes the reasons remain unclear.

Memories and moments: Positive memories of the person's life may be mixed with the sadness of their death. People will remember the good times they shared, their laughter, and their special moments together.

Stigma and social impact: Suicide can be surrounded by stigma. People may remember how society reacted to the loss. This might influence how they talk about the death or their hesitancy to discuss it openly.

Advocacy and support: Some individuals may be motivated to remember the person by advocating for mental health awareness and suicide prevention. They might channel their grief into supporting others struggling with similar issues.

Impact on human welfare: For those who were closest to the person who died by suicide, the event can have long-lasting effects on their mental health. They may experience grief, depression, anxiety, or other emotional challenges as they process the loss.

It is essential to remember that each person's experience with grief and the aftermath of a suicide is unique. If you or someone you know is struggling with thoughts of suicide or coping with the loss of a loved one to suicide, reaching out to mental health professionals, support groups, or helplines can provide crucial assistance and support.

You do not get over it and move on from grief. You are forced to make space for it. You carry it. You learn to live with it. And sometimes, you thrive despite it. Few of us ultimately escape the price we paid for loving deeply and profoundly. Make peace with losing people who did not show up for you and be in your corner when you needed them in your darkest hour. Acknowledge heavy truths and shift your mindset to embrace new beginnings. Stand alone, cry if you must, but never trust the wrong one again. You make your sympathies quite evident when you crave connection yet generate disconnection. Guard yourself when you are grieving, as many wolves will walk around you in sheep clothing. This will only add to your trauma. Healing is neither linear nor predictable; the pain and recovery will come in all shapes, sizes, and sources.

How does grief affect the brain? Neuroscientist Mary Frances O'Connor says, *"You cannot study grief without studying love."* Yvonne Bolton says, *"Love is physically encoded in the brain; our neurons help us to form an attachment to others. With the loss, the brain must come to terms with where our loved ones went or how to imagine a future that encompasses their absence."*

How can death affect your identity or confidence? Experts say identity rupture is a typical response to loss. People who are experiencing grief often ask themselves the following questions:

1. Who am I now without my mother/father/child/brother/sister/husband?

2. Who am I now without my career role?

3. How do I fit myself as a single person?

4. How do I continue life in a pod that has my sibling missing?

Our capacity to engage in the world and hope boundaries also change when we are grieving, says Lauren Brain, a professor of psychology. Grief is a shared aspect of humanity, but we do not do it well. But there is no time, and it is important to recognise your boundaries when you are out of control. Have a firm no and consider how much energy I have rather than pushing through, which I think people can often try to do.

Pain - the only way is through it. Psychologists Professor Gillian Straker and Dr. Jacqui Winship say the lesson is to go through the pain. The things you do to block your pain in the end are the things that harm you over time. It is the end of your physical relationship with them, but their memories and experiences continue to shape and influence us. Align the depths of your grief, and you will find that it is not bottomless.

My favourite authors, Glennon and Doyle, once said, *"Grief is the receipt we wave in the air that says to the world: Look! Love was once mine. I love well. Here is my proof that I paid the price."* Quote from the anthology Heart Warriors by Annie Gibbins, *"This is one of my favourite quotes because it explains that grief is proof of love. Grief represents the bond between the person's past and the person who has lost. The sheer complexity between grief and love is rife with opposition. However, in the end, pain values love. Whilst this is a simple formula layered with emotion, somewhere in there is a heart warrior who will turn to hope."* Here are some things that could help you manage your grief:

1. Ask your loved one to forgive you for not seeing any signs.

2. Forgive your loved one for the act of ending their life.

3. Be compassionate to yourself.

4. Seek the help of others, both professional and community.
5. Develop a sound support system as much as possible with friends and family.
6. Learn to support yourself with coping strategies.
7. Find and develop your tool kit.

It is processing the stages of grief, shock, denial, anger, bargaining, depression, acceptance, and hope. None of these stages are linear, and typically, people experiencing grief tend to return to stages, bounce between them, or sit in some longer than others. Never allow anyone to push you to process your grief according to their standards. Trauma is not just the bad stuff that happened. It is also the good paraphernalia that never occurred.

What if I told you that both wings belong to the same bird? Let it fly, even if the wings are clipped and sometimes broken. Your loved one is always part of you, no matter what circumstances prevail. Look at your failure standing beside you and behind you. Never let the ghosts of the past intimidate you. Create a poster for your present and your future self-talk. What you create will become your vista. Trauma responses are a shared experience that many people face in their lives, and they can have long-lasting effects on your mental and physical health. Understanding trauma responses can help us better cope with and heal from traumatic events. Trauma is a psychological and emotional response to an overwhelming or distressing event, and it can have a significant impact on an individual's mental, emotional, and even physical well-being. By learning about trauma responses, individuals and communities can gain insights into their reactions and those of others, fostering empathy and support during the healing process. Here are some key aspects of understanding trauma responses:

Fight: Anger that is controlling, the bully, judgement, slamming doors, and acting out aggressively.

Flight: Workaholic, overthinker, anxious, panicky, perfectionist, hyperactive, escaping or avoiding.

Fawn: People pleaser, no boundaries, lack of identity, co-dependent, seeking to please or appease others

Freeze: Feeling stuck, isolated, numb, shut down, and paralysed.

Friend: Trauma bonding with prolonged trauma, lack of identity, self-critique, and avoidance

Normalizing reactions: Traumatic events can trigger a wide range of responses, including fear, anxiety, sadness, anger, guilt, and shame. Understanding that these reactions are normal responses to an abnormal event can help individuals feel less isolated and "abnormal" themselves.

Triggers and flashbacks: Trauma can create triggers—stimuli or situations that remind individuals of the traumatic event, eliciting intense emotional and physiological reactions. Flashbacks, on the other hand, are vivid and distressing recollections of the traumatic event. Identifying triggers and understanding flashbacks can empower individuals to manage their responses better.

Dissociation: Traumatic events can lead to dissociation, where individuals mentally disconnect from their thoughts, feelings, memories, or sense of identity to protect themselves from overwhelming emotions. Recognizing dissociation can be crucial in seeking appropriate support.

Secondary trauma: This refers to the indirect trauma experienced by those who are exposed to the traumatic experiences of others, such as first responders, healthcare providers, or family members of victims. Understanding secondary trauma can help build empathy and encourage self-care for those providing support.

Resilience and coping: Recognizing that trauma can have long-lasting effects, individuals can focus on building resilience and healthy coping mechanisms to navigate the healing process effectively.

Seeking professional support: Trauma can be complex, and professional help from therapists, counsellors, or support groups can provide the guidance and tools needed for healing.

Self-compassion: Understanding trauma responses also involves being compassionate with oneself and recognizing that healing takes time. Avoiding self-blame and negative self-judgment is crucial for the recovery process.

By increasing awareness and understanding of trauma responses, individuals and communities can create a more supportive and empathetic environment, enabling survivors to cope with and heal from their traumatic experiences more effectively. Never dress and rehearse the trauma to beat vulnerability. You will squander your peace. One can never predict what happens after trauma; understand the element of uncertainty.

Acknowledge the pain: The first step in healing past trauma is to acknowledge the pain you have experienced because it is essential to recognize the emotions and memories associated with the traumatic event. Permit yourself to feel, as suppressing or denying these emotions can prolong healing. Ultimately, all healing starts with self-compassion, and we can only show compassion for something we acknowledge. Healing past trauma through self-forgiveness is a transformative and empowering process. By accepting the pain, practising self-compassion, and releasing guilt, you can gradually release the burdens that have held you back. Remember, healing takes time and patience, but with dedication and self-love, you can reclaim your emotional freedom and create a brighter future. Remember to embrace self-forgiveness as a powerful tool to heal, grow, and thrive. Here are a few points to remember on your healing journey:

- It is all about your state of mind rather than letting others off the hook.
- Understand the nature of forgiveness; forgiveness does not imply condoning or forgetting the actions that caused the trauma.
- Letting go of resentment, anger, and bitterness is a personal choice.
- Understand that forgiving yourself is not an act of weakness but rather an act of empowerment and self-love.
- Recognize that forgiving yourself is for your well-being, allowing you to move forward without being held captive by the past.

Practice self-compassion: Self-compassion is crucial in the journey of self-forgiveness. Treat yourself with kindness and understanding, just as you would support a dear friend. Acknowledge that you are a human being capable of making mistakes and experiencing pain. Be patient and gentle with yourself throughout the healing process.

Release the burden of guilt: Guilt often accompanies past trauma, as we blame ourselves for the events that occurred. However, it is important to realize that guilt is an unproductive and burdensome emotion that hinders healing, so be sure to reflect on the circumstances surrounding the trauma, understanding that you did the best you could with the knowledge and resources available at that time. Accept that you cannot change the past but can change how you respond to it and see the future.

Engage in self-reflection: Self-reflection is a powerful tool for healing. Take time to examine your past actions, thoughts, and beliefs that may have contributed to the trauma. Seek to understand yourself and the factors that influenced your decisions. By gaining insight into your motivations and vulnerabilities, you can foster personal growth and prevent similar situations in the future.

Practice mindfulness and meditation: Mindfulness and meditation can aid in healing past trauma by fostering self-awareness and emotional regulation. These practices help cultivate a non-judgmental and accepting attitude towards your thoughts and emotions. By observing your thoughts without attachment, you can gradually detach from the negative feelings associated with past trauma and develop a sense of inner peace.

Seek support: Healing past trauma can be a challenging journey, and it's crucial to seek support from trusted individuals or experts who have gone through similar struggles. This can provide validation, understanding, and valuable insights.

Before looking for the lesson in the struggle, remember to slow down and have some compassion for yourself. I see too many people offering advice to find the lesson in the pain way too quickly. Processing and allowing yourself to feel the pain are important part of the healing journey. Do not rush or push through the process; it will create more pain than you realise. Pushing through may seem heroic, but it is more damaging to your psyche and physical well-being in the long run. Take your time with your healing journey; you are worth it.

The effects of suicide, grief, and trauma on GDP (Gross Domestic Product) are complex and not straightforward to quantify. These issues can have both direct and indirect impacts on economic productivity and well-being:

Direct economic impact: Suicide, grief, and trauma can lead to direct economic costs. For instance, there are medical costs associated with treating injuries resulting from suicide attempts, costs of funeral services and bereavement support for families affected by suicide, and expenses related to trauma counselling and mental health care. These costs can strain healthcare systems and social services, leading to financial burdens on individuals and governments alike.

Lost productivity: The emotional toll of grief and trauma can significantly affect an individual's ability to work or be productive. Grieving individuals may experience difficulties concentrating, decreased motivation, and increased absenteeism. Similarly, those directly impacted by traumatic events may face challenges in resuming regular work duties, leading to workforce productivity loss.

Long-term impact: Grief and trauma can have long-lasting effects on individuals and communities. Prolonged grief or post-traumatic stress disorder (PTSD) may lead to chronic health issues, long work absences, or early retirement. These factors can reduce an individual's contribution to the economy and potentially increase their reliance on disability benefits or social welfare programs.

Decreased consumer spending: Communities impacted by suicide, grief, or trauma may experience a decline in consumer spending. Individuals and families dealing with emotional distress may reduce discretionary spending, reducing demand for goods and services in the affected areas.

Impact on human capital: Suicide and trauma can rob societies of valuable human capital. The loss of life through suicide can have far-reaching effects on families, friends, and communities. Additionally, trauma experienced during critical developmental stages, such as childhood, can affect educational attainment and future job opportunities, potentially reducing a country's human capital potential.

Stigma and workplace climate: In some cases, the stigma surrounding mental health issues may discourage individuals from seeking help, leading to continued suffering and decreased productivity in the workplace. A lack of supportive workplace environments can further exacerbate the effects of grief and trauma on employees' well-being and performance.

It is important to note that while the impacts of suicide, grief, and trauma on GDP can be significant, the human toll and suffering associated with these issues are immeasurable. Addressing human welfare challenges and providing appropriate support for those affected by suicide and trauma should be a priority for society beyond just considering their economic consequences. Preventing suicide, promoting mental well-being, and providing effective grief and trauma support can have positive effects not only on individuals and families but also on the overall economic health and productivity of a nation. Investment in mental health services, counselling, and community support can lead to a more resilient and productive society. There will always be offences or sensitive moments in life. Realise that life does not have to be perfect; start living your abundant life in all circumstances.

Unprocessed grief is a profound and often overwhelming emotional experience that occurs when an individual fails to adequately address and come to terms with their loss. It is a complex and lingering sensation, like a heavy weight that remains in one's heart and mind. When grief is left unprocessed, it can manifest in various ways, such as prolonged sadness, anger, guilt, or even physical symptoms. It becomes a silent companion, shaping one's thoughts, behaviours, and relationships. Unprocessed grief can hinder personal growth and the ability to move forward in life, making it crucial for individuals to seek support and embrace the healing process to find solace and peace in the face of their loss. Unprocessed grief is like an emotional weight that lingers in the depths of one's soul, refusing to be acknowledged or released.

Common Grief Emotions:

Grief Shock: Surprise, disbelief, shock, horror, feeling numb - as if your spirit has 'split' from your body.

Emotional Release: Crying - daily, weekly, fortnightly, monthly; shed a few tears, whimper, snivel, cry, weep, sob, howl,

Grief Depression: Sadness, misery, unhappiness, suicidal ideation, self-harm, attempting suicide, completing suicide

Grief (Physical) Illness: Mild illness, mild aches, and pains. What are some of the symptoms?

Grief Panic: Afraid, dreaded, scared, terrified, alarmed, panicky, feeling of wanting to run away

Grief Guilt: 'If only,' imagined guilt, feeling shame, blaming oneself/others, remorse, real guilt, guilty consciousness, culpability

Grief Apathy: 'Feeling slack,' a pattern of sickness, lack of energy, tiredness, lack of concern, lack of interest, weary, exhaustion, apathetic, not caring, may neglect family, friends, colleagues, and work

Grief Anger: Irritable, passive-aggressive, nasty, aggressive, spiteful, holding grudges, angry, malice, violent

The silent pain festers beneath the surface, often hidden behind a facade of strength or indifference. When we fail to confront and work through our grief, it can manifest in unexpected and destructive ways, affecting our mental, emotional, and even physical well-being. Unprocessed grief may lead to prolonged feelings of sadness, anger, or emptiness, and it can interfere with our ability to form meaningful connections and move forward in life. Like an unresolved chapter in a book, unprocessed grief keeps us stuck in the past, preventing us from fully embracing the present and looking towards the future with hope and healing. It is only through the courageous act of acknowledging and processing our grief that we can find solace and the opportunity to rebuild our lives with newfound strength and resilience.

To begin our journey, we must understand what trauma is and how it affects us. Trauma can be physical, emotional, or psychological, and it often leaves lasting scars. By recognizing the nature of your trauma and acknowledging its impact, you can start the healing process. Healing from trauma is a challenging journey, and it is crucial to seek support from a qualified therapist or counsellor. They can provide the tools and guidance you need to work through your trauma effectively. Remember, you do not have to go through this process alone. Self-compassion is a cornerstone of healing. It would be best if you learned to be kind and forgiving to yourself. Understand that it is okay to feel the way you do, and that healing takes time. Self-compassion can help you break free from self-blame and guilt. Resilience is your superpower. As you heal, focus on building your resilience. This involves developing coping strategies, setting healthy boundaries, and nurturing physical and mental well-being. Resilience will empower you to face life's challenges with strength.

Mindfulness is a powerful tool for healing. By staying in the present moment and observing your thoughts and emotions without judgment, you can gain control over your reactions and reduce the impact of your trauma. Practising mindfulness through meditation and self-awareness can be transformative. Trauma often affects our relationships. Work on rebuilding trust with loved ones and forming new connections as you heal. Open and honest communication is vital to repairing bonds and creating a support system that sustains your healing journey. Finding meaning in your life can be a driving force for transcending trauma. Consider your values and passions and explore how you can contribute positively to the world. Meaning and purpose can provide a sense of direction and motivation.

Forgiveness is a complex but liberating step. It does not mean condoning the actions that caused your trauma; it means releasing the power those actions hold over you. Forgiving others and, more importantly, forgiving yourself can be a transformative experience. Your trauma does not define your story. By reshaping your narrative, you can find empowerment and hope. Revisit your life's experiences and highlight moments of strength and resilience. You are the author of your life; you can change its direction.

Transcending trauma is not about erasing the past; it is about moving beyond it. As you work through the previous chapters, you will find yourself on a path to transcendence. Your trauma will no longer define you but rather serve as a chapter in your story, making you stronger, wiser, and more compassionate. Healing from trauma is a courageous and transformative journey. It takes time, effort, and patience, but the destination is worth every step. Remember that you are not alone; countless individuals have transcended trauma to find peace, happiness, and a renewed sense of purpose. As you walk this path, may you find healing, growth, and the strength to live a life filled with love and joy.

Image 11: Photo of Jayandra and Kelly taken in Sydney, Australia, in 2016.

Grief can be the garden of compassion. If you keep your heart open through everything, the pain can become your greatest ally. Search for love and wisdom." - Rumi.

12. Afterlife and Consciousness

After the suicide of Jayandra, I grappled with many things as many themes eluded my sleep. As a Christian, I constantly pondered about the destination of his soul. Many people constantly reiterated that it was his time to die, and this angered me. When your existence is splintered like a dry, sharp piece of wood, is this your time to die? The collective trauma from this saga is still pumping in my veins. Crystallized in everyone's consciousness is a carnival of different cultures and beliefs. I had no comfort but tears, and then I researched the matter. What happens when a loved one dies from suicide?

Nirvana in Buddhism represents a state of enlightenment and liberation from the cycle of birth and death. The existence of an afterlife is a matter of faith and personal belief, as there is currently no scientific evidence to support or refute the concept. Consciousness is the state of being aware of and able to perceive one's surroundings, thoughts, emotions, and experiences. It is a fundamental aspect of human existence and is central to our subjective world experience. However, the nature of consciousness and how it arises from the brain remain one of the greatest mysteries in science and philosophy. The scientific study of consciousness involves various disciplines, such as neuroscience, psychology, and philosophy. While significant progress has been made in understanding how certain brain structures and processes correlate with specific conscious experiences, the exact mechanisms by which subjective awareness arises are not fully understood.

The study of altered states of consciousness, such as during meditation, drug-induced experiences, or near-death experiences, also adds complexity to the understanding of consciousness.

Afterlife and consciousness are complex and multifaceted topics. Afterlife is a matter of religious and cultural belief, while consciousness is a subject of ongoing scientific investigation and philosophical enquiry. As our understanding of the human mind and brain continues to evolve, these topics will likely remain subjects of great interest and debate. It is important to note that the question of what happens after death is ultimately a matter of belief and speculation, as no empirical evidence conclusively supports any one view.

Hindu beliefs about the soul after death are rooted in reincarnation, which is the belief that the soul is eternal and undergoes a cycle of birth, death, and rebirth. This cycle is known as *"samsara."* The specific beliefs can vary across different schools of Hindu thought. Still, there are some common principles:

Reincarnation: Hindus believe that after death, the soul leaves the body and enters a new one, starting a new life. The next life's circumstances, including species, family, and social position, are determined by the accumulated karma of the previous life.

Karma: Is the law of cause and effect. It governs the consequences of one's actions, thoughts, and intentions. Good actions lead to positive outcomes, while wrong actions lead to negative ones. The accumulation of karma in one life influences the circumstances of the next. Consciousness is reborn into a new physical body based on past actions and karma.

Moksha: The ultimate goal for many Hindus is to break free from the cycle of birth and death (samsara) and attain liberation, or "moksha." Achieving moksha means the soul unites with the divine or cosmic consciousness, transcending the cycle of rebirth and experiencing eternal bliss and liberation from suffering.

Afterlife realms: Hinduism describes various realms or planes where souls can go after death based on their karma. These realms include heaven (Swarga) for those who have accumulated good karma and hellish realms (Naraka) for those with negative karma. However, these realms are considered temporary and not the final destination.

Ancestors and Pitru-loka: Hindus also believe in ancestor worship and perform rituals to honour deceased ancestors. The souls of ancestors are believed to reside in the realm called "Pitru-loka" or the world of ancestors, and their blessings and guidance are sought for the well-being of the living.

Funeral rites and ceremonies: Hindu funeral rites vary across regions and sects, but they generally involve cremating the body and performing various rituals to ensure the peaceful journey of the departed soul to the next realm and to support its transition. It is important to note that while these are common beliefs among Hindus, there is a diverse range of beliefs and practices within the Hindu faith, and interpretations may vary among individuals and different schools of thought.

The Bible does not explicitly address the fate of a person's soul after death by suicide. Different Christian denominations have varied interpretations, and opinions may vary among theologians and believers. It is important to approach this sensitive topic with compassion and understanding. In Christianity, suicide is generally considered a sin because it involves the taking of one's own life, and many Christian traditions teach that all human life is sacred and should be respected. The Ten Commandments include the commandment *"You shall not murder"* (Exodus 20:13), which is often interpreted to encompass taking one's own life as well.

Some Christians believe that if a person dies by suicide, they may still find forgiveness and salvation through God's mercy and grace. Others, however, may feel that suicide is an act of self-murder and that such an act can lead to spiritual consequences. Ultimately, the Bible emphasizes that God is the ultimate judge of our hearts and actions. Only God knows the full extent of someone's struggles, circumstances, and mental state, and He alone can determine a person's eternal destiny. Christians are encouraged to show empathy and support to those who are struggling with mental health issues or thoughts of suicide, to offer love, compassion, and understanding, and to seek professional help for those in need. The focus is often on providing hope, healing, and comfort to those who have been affected by the loss of a loved one to suicide rather than making definitive pronouncements about the eternal fate of their souls.

Is suicide a sin? This is one of the subjects of questions where the answer depends on your personal morals and religious beliefs. What does the Bible say about suicide? Author George Howe Colt states in *November of the Soul*, *"Considering Christianity's nearly two thousand years of intense opposition to suicide, it is surprising that neither* the *Old nor New Testament directly prohibits the act."* Both testaments combined only reveal a small percentage of suicide stories, and these are recorded with no judgment.

Other philosophical and scientific perspectives suggest that death is the end of our existence. They propose that once the body and brain cease functioning, our consciousness and sense of self cease to exist. **"I was ashamed of myself when I realised life was a costume party, and I attended with my real face." - Franz Kafka.** Still, after all this time, the sun never declares to the earth that you are in debt to me. Look at the reciprocal relationship—a profound love that ignites the sky and sustains the planet. Get strategic about creating symbiotic relationships in your life. When you make personal choices, always remember that you are a tripod being: mind, body, and soul. Let your decisions liberate all three dimensions of your existence.

In recent times, there has been a growing emphasis on understanding mental health and the complexities that lead to suicide. Many societies are moving away from stigmatizing individuals who have died by suicide and are focusing on providing support, empathy, and resources for those struggling with mental health issues. It is essential to approach this topic sensitively and respect different beliefs and perspectives. If you or someone you know is struggling with thoughts of suicide, it is crucial to seek help from mental health professionals, counsellors, or helplines that specialize in providing support for such situations.

The concept of the soul as imperishable has been a central tenet of many philosophical and religious traditions throughout history. It asserts that the essence of an individual, often considered the seat of one's consciousness and identity, is eternal and transcends the physical realm. This belief suggests that the soul continues to exist beyond the confines of our earthly existence, persisting even after the body's death. Various faiths, from Hinduism's belief in reincarnation to Christianity's notion of everlasting life, embrace the idea that the soul is not perishable. Such beliefs provide solace and hope, offering the prospect of an enduring connection with the universe, the divine, or a higher purpose beyond the temporal boundaries of human existence.

You work eight hours to live four.
You work six days to enjoy one.
You work eight hours to eat in 15 minutes.
You work eight hours to sleep five
You work all year just to take a week or two of vacation.
You work all your life to retire in old age.
And contemplate only your last breaths.

Eventually, you realise that life is a parody of yourself practising for your oblivion. We have become so accustomed to material and social slavery that we no longer see the chains. Life is a short journey; live it. Collect memories, not material things.

To live the life of your soul is not easy. However, you make it more difficult than it is. Your soul's life is a journey where we face ourselves every day. We face ourselves through the reflections of others and the reflections of ourselves in a mirror. If you prefer to live abundantly and make earnest investments in your soul, think outside the box of just here and now. Understand what the implications are for your soul as well. Only you can decide whether you want to exist or live.

You start dying gradually...
When you never travel
Refuse to read
Reject correction
Throw away introspection.

You start dying gradulally...
Once you slay your self-esteem
When your own kin know nothing about you
While you feed someone, and they poison you
Formerly gaslighted by your loved one.

You start dying gradually...
When you navigate the same paths and expect a different result
Rebel to never change the narrative
Shy away from purging your circle
When you numb yourself just to endure life.

You have already begun to die gradually, yet no one cares to notice. You are the only person who will compassionately understand your journey and plight. Never let yourself die unconsciously or consciously. Live every day with passion and purpose despite the circumstances. Grief and trauma do not keep a schedule; they just show up unannounced. You cannot kill it with a brick. If wishes were horses, beggars would ride. A worthy life is crafted; get strategic and create a visual fortitude to advocate for your future and dreams.

"Hesed" (also spelled "chesed" or "chesid") is a Hebrew word found in the Old Testament of the Bible. **It often describes God's steadfast, loyal, and covenantal love for His people.** Hesed embodies a deep and enduring love characterized by kindness, mercy, faithfulness, and compassion. It goes beyond fleeting emotions and is committed to upholding promises and maintaining a loving relationship. In human relationships, "hesed" encourages believers to extend this same kind of steadfast love and faithfulness to others, reflecting the divine nature of God's love. Here are a few ways to embody "hesed" love in your actions based on its biblical principles:

Faithful commitment: Just as God remains faithful to His covenant promises, you can demonstrate "hesed" love by being committed and loyal in your relationships, keeping your promises, and standing by others even in challenging times.

Kindness and compassion: Show kindness and compassion to others, especially when they are in need or facing difficulties. Offer your support, care, and understanding as a tangible expression of love.

Forgiveness and mercy: Just as God extends forgiveness and mercy, practice forgiveness towards others who may have wronged you. Letting go of grudges and extending grace can cultivate an atmosphere of "hesed" love.

Generosity: Be generous with your time, resources, and help. Meeting the needs of others, whether material or emotional, is an act of love that reflects the selfless nature of "hesed."

Consistency: "Hesed" love is not based on fleeting emotions but endures over time. Strive to consistently show care, concern, and affection to those around you.

Support and encouragement: Provide support and encouragement to those struggling or discouraged. Your words of affirmation and acts of support can uplift and strengthen others.

Maintain relationships: "Hesed" love emphasizes maintaining relationships even in the face of challenges. Work through disagreements, communicate openly, and seek reconciliation when needed.

Seek reconciliation: When conflicts arise, take the initiative to seek reconciliation and restore harmony. This reflects the reconciling nature of God's "hesed" love.

Prayerful intercession: Pray for the well-being and needs of others, just as you would pray for yourself. Interceding on behalf of others is a powerful expression of love.

Selflessness: Place the needs and interests of others above your desires. Sacrificing your comfort or preferences for the sake of others reflects the selfless nature of "hesed."

By embodying the principles of "hesed" love in your actions and relationships, you can contribute to a world where kindness, faithfulness, and compassion prevail, reflecting the divine nature of God's unwavering love for His people. This also confirms God's love for Jayandra and all other suicide victims. They are at God's mercy because of His hesed love for them. The reality is that we all end up in a grave that is approximately the same dimension or as ashes dispersed somewhere. After a chess game, the king and the soldier are stored in the same box. There is no distinction between position, hierarchy, post, title, status, or honour. All this is temporary, and the same is applicable in life. Stop strutting your stuff. What people take to the grave as a permanent life tattoo is how you treat them. What you did for them in their greatest hour of need and how you read between the lines to understand what made them tick. How and when did you offer solace and comfort to a bleeding heart?

"You will never reach your destination if you stop and throw stones at every dog that barks." - Winston Churchill.

Conclusion

"The Life of Jayandra" is a testament to the light and darkness we carry. The resilience of the human spirit and the power of compassion and understanding in the bleakest seasons of life. It also shines a light on characters that refuse to walk in the light—those who ultimately push others to the edge and are happy to see them jump off the cliff. By shedding light on the topic of suicide and addressing it with empathy and knowledge, it may reduce stigma, increase awareness, and ultimately save lives. With the proper support, resources, and commitment to mental health and human welfare, we can all create a world where individuals feel empowered to speak out, find hope, and rediscover the beauty of life. Let us embark on a journey into the light and regenerate a brighter future together. In addition, society needs to stop sugarcoating lousy behaviour, and humanity needs to recognise a spade as a spade. Turning a blind eye to poor conduct will taint the ecosystem infinitely.

Remember, you are always responsible for how you act, no matter how you feel. Some of the worst people in the Bible made the most positive impact. Simply because their story did not end with their mistake, it finished with their comeback. You may feel like you are on a lost course, but remember it is not over; your victory is your choice. Some people were not put here to evolve. They are here to remind you what it looks like if you do not. People have a knack for selling their dreams and delivering nightmares. Never allow the agenda of others to derail your life. Heard melodies and memories are sweet, but those unheard are sweeter. Jayandra, your cherished memories will never be forgotten. You are like a book; most people only saw your cover, a minority read only the introduction, some flicked through the pages but did not care to read, many believed in the critics, and very few ever knew your content.

I did not understand the profound magnitude of this, but I do now. My brother Jayandra gave me one of the most important lessons of my life. Perseverance amidst brokenness, life may alter and change, but it still prevails. As the seasons changed and tossed him into inclement conditions, he navigated to a brighter day. I will always salute you, Jayandra, for modelling life to me without even knowing what an impeccable example you were. I shudder to think of how I would have charted life if I had dwelled in your shoes, even for a day. You are a mighty warrior. Courage is not always strong. It is embellished in everyday life by simply showing up, even as a disabled person with no employment or secured future.

I have the urge to tell you about my day, my brother...
I long for you to answer the phone when I call...
I want to laugh with you...
I desire to hear about your day...

I crave to create memories with you...
You still show me you care in magnificent ways...
I honour you in your tolerance and defiance...
However, all the days start and end the same...

Each day now begins and ends without you...
This is the narrative for eternity...
We shared the same womb and a little of life...
I respect your courage and delicacy...

You left by choice, and it hurts...
You will always be a voice in my ear and a beat in my heart...
I am loyal to retaining the truth of your essence...
Until I see you in heaven, and then we will smile again!

My dear friend and reader:

In times of uncertainty and darkness, I wish to share a message of hope. Although life can be filled with challenges and hardships, it is essential to remember that hope can be found even in the darkest moments. Hope is the flame that continues to burn within our hearts, guiding us through difficult times. It is the beacon that lights our path when all seems lost. Hope whispers to us that better days are ahead and reminds us to hold on to our dreams, no matter how distant they may seem. In times of adversity, hope gives us the strength to endure, rise above our circumstances, and find solutions to our problems. It empowers us to be resilient and to see opportunities where others might only see obstacles.

Hope can unite us as a community, reminding us that we are not alone in our struggles. It fosters compassion, empathy, and support, encouraging us to reach out to others and offer a helping hand.

Remember that even in the face of adversity, there is always a chance for positive change. History has shown us that humanity is capable of tremendous resilience and progress, overcoming challenges that once seemed insurmountable. As you navigate your journey, hold onto hope tightly and let it be your guiding light. Embrace the belief that we can create a brighter, more compassionate, and more harmonious world. Remember, my friend, that hope is not just wishful thinking; it is the foundation upon which we can build a better future for ourselves and future generations. May hope fill your heart and empower you to face whatever lies ahead with courage and determination. Together, let us spread hope to all those who need it, lighting the world with positivity and love.

With hope and warm regards,
Author, Kelly Markey
Reach out if you need a beacon of hope, light, or inspiration.
KellyMarkey.com

Understand this: bad chapters can still create stories. Wrong paths can still lead to the right places. Failed dreams can still make successful people. Sometimes, it takes losing yourself to find yourself. Hurt people hurt others. However, healed people can heal others. Safe people shelter others. Free spirits liberate others. Enlightened people illuminate others. Love always wins. Shine your light of love on all who may come across your path in life because what you do matters. Start filling your cup, understanding what contents you prefer, loving your skin, cherishing your existence, validating your journey, speaking your truth, admiring your reflection, enjoying your company, and creating your paradise. Excellence is never an accident. It is always the result of high intention, sincere effort, and intelligent execution. Address what is wrong, and if parties prefer to play the ostrich syndrome, rest assured that you have done your due diligence.

Excerpt from the chapter that I co-authored from the book *Heart Warrior*. *"Performance requires professionalism. I contributed professionally despite my broken emotions. What did your warrior define? Bifurcation is the process of splitting something into two. For example, bifurcation allows one to get divorced while leaving property issues to be settled later. When the day, project, team, manager, life or the world seem overwhelming, recall and lean into the bifurcation process to deal only with what you have the energy for. The rest will find itself on your future agenda. Take a page from this process and focus on the fundamental task while you manage the rest later. Remember, a warrior is not crafted by default, but instead leads with that wholesome heart grounded by the true character, not the pecking order of a profession."* Learn that some people are loyal to nothing but a pay cheque even if you are fragmented, adopt the bifurcation process, and prioritise your welfare. You can shelf everything else for later.

The most substantial advantage—the genius of living - is never to pay the ultimate price with your life. Especially when life has a circuitous route, some players are James Bond witty and charming but have no respect for your welfare. Never hand them the keys to your life. Understanding how to process anger is important for maintaining emotional well-being and healthy relationships. Here are some effective ways to handle and process anger:

Recognize and acknowledge your anger: It is essential to be aware of your emotions and not suppress or deny them. Recognise when you are angry and accept that it is valid.

Take a break: When you feel anger rising, step back from the situation. Give yourself some time and space to cool down before you react.

Deep breathing and relaxation: Practice breathing or other relaxation techniques like meditation to calm your mind and body. This can help you regain composure and think more clearly.

Identify triggers and patterns: Reflect on what triggers your anger and try to understand the underlying patterns. Awareness of your triggers can help you manage your responses better.

Express your feelings: Find healthy ways to express your anger. You can talk to a friend, family member, or therapist about what is bothering you. Writing in a journal can also be a helpful outlet.

Use "I" statements: When discussing your anger with someone, use "I" statements to express your feelings without blaming or attacking them. For example, say, "I felt hurt when..." instead of, "You always make me angry when..."

Practice empathy: See the situation from the other person's perspective. Understanding their viewpoint can diffuse some of your anger and open the door to constructive communication.

Avoid aggression: Avoid aggressive or violent responses to anger. Instead, focus on assertive communication and finding solutions to the issues at hand.

Physical activity: Physical activities like exercise, sports, or yoga can help release built-up tension and reduce anger.

Seek professional help: If you find that anger is significantly impacting your life and relationships, consider seeking support from a therapist or counsellor who specializes in anger management.

Practice forgiveness: Holding onto anger can be detrimental to your mental well-being. Try to practice forgiveness, not for the other person's sake but for your peace of mind.

Establish healthy boundaries: Sometimes, anger can arise when our boundaries are crossed. Learn to set and communicate your boundaries clearly to prevent future conflicts.

Remember, anger is a natural emotion, and it is okay to feel it. The key is to handle it in a way that does not cause harm to yourself or others. Developing healthy anger management skills takes time and practice, but with persistence, you can learn to process anger constructively and positively.

Change is not easy. It is meant to rip up your roots and cultivate a new side where your roots can deepen. It is going to be okay in the long run. What you may perceive as regret can become a lesson; what made you bitter can make you better if you only focus on what you have learned rather than dwell on the pain it dispensed. Do not be encouraged by false positivity. Be sad when you are sad. Cry if you need to. Be angry if you feel angry.

Let it out. Then let it go. Acknowledge your emotions, but always choose to dwell on the positive ones. Never stagnate with negative emotions. Heal your soul by letting go of your emotional addictions. You can never build a kingdom with someone who still craves attention from the village. You can move past things and people that no longer bring positivity to your life. Be willing to believe in the positive, even if you do not like it. Trust the timing and be patient; everything will unravel in time. Always pay attention to the lessons that life has taught you. Sometimes, you will be presented with the same thing in a different package to test if you have learned. *"Awakening is not changing who you are but discarding who you are not." - Deepak Chopra.*

The statement, *"The final stage of healing is using what happens to you to help others,"* conveys a profound idea about the transformative power of personal experiences. It suggests that after going through a healing process, individuals can reach a stage where they can use their own experiences, struggles, and growth to benefit others who may be going through similar challenges. The concept behind this idea is that healing is not just about finding relief from pain or distress; it also involves a deeper understanding of oneself and others. When someone goes through a healing journey and overcomes their difficulties, they gain valuable insights, empathy, and wisdom that can be shared with others facing similar circumstances.

By helping others, individuals can find a sense of purpose and fulfilment, knowing that their experiences were not in vain and can be used to positively impact the lives of others. Giving back and supporting others on their paths of healing can create a positive ripple effect, fostering a sense of community, compassion, and mutual understanding. It is important to note that healing is a personal process, and individuals may reach different stages of healing at different times. While some people might feel ready to help others early in their journey, others might need more time to focus on their recovery before extending a helping hand. Moreover, not everyone may use their experiences to help others directly, which is perfectly valid. Healing is a unique and individual process, and each person should honour their own pace and preferences. Ultimately, using one's experiences to help others emphasizes the power of empathy, human connection, and the potential for personal growth and positive change in the world.

The art of endurance refers to the ability to persevere and withstand challenging situations over an extended period. Endurance is a valuable trait that applies to various aspects of life, including the physical, mental, emotional, and spiritual realms. Whether you are an athlete, a student, an entrepreneur, or simply dealing with life's ups and downs, cultivating endurance can lead to tremendous success, growth, and resilience. Here are some key elements of endurance:

Mindset: Endurance begins with the right mindset. Maintaining a positive and determined attitude is crucial, even in the face of obstacles. It involves believing in yourself, your abilities, and your capacity to overcome difficulties.

Goal Setting: Setting clear and achievable goals provides a sense of purpose and direction. Breaking down significant goals into smaller, manageable steps allows you to track progress and stay motivated.

Perseverance: Endurance requires unwavering persistence. It is about not giving up when faced with setbacks or failures but instead using them as learning opportunities and steppingstones to improvement.

Self-discipline: Developing self-discipline is essential to enduring challenges. It means staying focused on your goals, making consistent efforts, and maintaining good habits even when the going gets tough.

Emotional intelligence: Being emotionally aware and effectively managing your emotions can help you navigate challenging times and maintain a balanced outlook.

Physical endurance: Physical endurance involves building stamina and strength through regular exercise and a healthy lifestyle. Taking care of your body contributes to mental and emotional resilience as well.

Time management: Effectively managing your time ensures that you stay on track and not become overwhelmed by competing priorities.

Adaptability: Endurance does not mean being rigid; it also involves being adaptable and open to change. Life is full of surprises, and flexibility can help you navigate uncertain situations.

Seeking support: Endurance does not mean you must go through everything alone. Seeking support from friends, family, mentors, or professionals can provide encouragement and valuable insights.

Focus on the process: While goals are essential, focusing solely on the result can be overwhelming. Embrace the process, enjoy the journey, and celebrate small victories.

Resilience: Endurance and resilience go hand in hand. Resilience allows you to bounce back from adversity and continue moving forward.

Learning from failures: Embrace failure as a part of the process. View it as a chance to learn and grow rather than a reason to quit.

Ultimately, endurance involves embracing challenges, staying committed to your goals, and consistently putting in the effort required to overcome obstacles. It is not about being invincible but rather about developing the strength to persist in the face of adversity and emerge stronger on the other side.

Make yourself a priority. You are your most extended commitment. If you remember anything about me after I leave this world, recall that I loved you even when it was foolish. I cared even when it was unwarranted. When my body is gone, remember my heart, the spirit of Jayandra. The bravest are those who can choose the future regardless of the present colours of life. The mildest touch changes the eons for the future. Give anything time, and it will take care of itself: karma, cosmos, vindication, contriving, prayers, or simply doing nothing. The tide will eventually turn as sure as the sun rises every morning. Exhale, this is just a chapter, not the conclusion. No fire can be put out unless everyone grabs a bucket.

When I am gone
Recall, I ran my race with the cards dealt
Remember not my woes
Memorise only my smile

Forget the unkind that I have sown
Consider the noble I have done
Dwell not on the sorrow I planted
Reminisce on the blessings that I scattered

Disregard when I have faltered and goofed
Bring to remembrance the battles that I fought and won
Overlook the grief and trauma after I am gone
Let the incense and flowers remind you where,
my final resting place is

When dusk paints the sky
Come stand a few moments beside me
As you remember my heartbeat
Retain only my best memories

As you release a tear
I discharge a smile as I appreciate that you now
know my tears
Let it be well with both our souls!

Jayandra, it was a privilege to share life with you. Your warmth, kindness, unwavering support and constant smiles despite your circumstances was an impeccable example to me. Your love and influence will remain an eternal beacon.

Image 12: Photo taken in Sydney, Australia, in 2016.

"Never be afraid to raise your voice for honesty, truth, and compassion against injustice, lying, and greed. If people all over the world do this, it would change the world." - William Faulkner.

Tool 1. Tools to Navigate to a Better Season

(For those struggling with suicidal thoughts)

Navigating to a better season in life often requires a combination of self-awareness, personal development, and practical tools. Here are some tools and strategies to help you move towards a more positive and fulfilling season:

Goal setting: Define clear and achievable short-term and long-term goals. Break them into smaller, manageable tasks to maintain motivation and track progress.

Positive mindset: Cultivate a positive outlook on life by focusing on gratitude, affirmations, and positive self-talk. Challenge negative thought patterns and replace them with constructive ones.

Self-reflection: Regularly reflect on your experiences, emotions, and reactions. Journaling can be a helpful tool for self-discovery and understanding your feelings.

Support network: Surround yourself with supportive and positive individuals. Share your challenges and successes with trusted friends and family members or seek guidance from a mentor or therapist.

Mindfulness and meditation: Practice mindfulness to stay present and reduce stress. Meditation can also help you gain clarity and find peace amidst life's challenges.

Healthy habits: Focus on physical well-being by maintaining a balanced diet, regular exercise, and adequate sleep. A healthy body can positively impact your mental state.

Limit negative influences: Identify negative influences in your life, whether toxic relationships, unhealthy habits, or excessive exposure to negative media. Limit or remove them from your life to create space for positivity.

Skill development: Invest time in learning new skills or honing existing ones. Expanding your knowledge can boost your confidence and open new opportunities.

Time management: Organize your time effectively by setting priorities and avoiding procrastination. This will help you stay focused and reduce stress.

Visualization: Use visualization techniques to imagine your desired outcomes and manifest positive changes in your life.

Flexibility and adaptability: Embrace change and be willing to adapt your plans when necessary. Life is dynamic, and flexibility can help you navigate uncertain times.

Seek professional help: If you are struggling with emotional or mental health challenges, do not hesitate to seek support from a therapist or counsellor.

Volunteer and give back: Contributing to your community or helping others in need can give you a sense of purpose and fulfilment.

Limit comparison: Avoid constant comparison with others. Focus on your growth and journey, acknowledging that everyone has their unique path.

Celebrate progress: Acknowledge and celebrate your achievements, no matter how small. Positive reinforcement can boost your motivation.

Remember, navigating to a better season takes time and effort. Be patient with yourself and allow for setbacks. Progress may be gradual, but with consistent effort and the right tools, you can create positive changes in your life.

Thousands of people with anxiety are living testimonies that a person can live a productive and satisfying life even with significant periods of distress. What can you do to reduce the intensity, persistence, and adverse effects of anxiety in your life? A combination of strategies is available that address both the underlying causes and the immediate symptoms. Here are some effective ways to manage anxiety:

1. Exercise regularly
2. Limit caffeine and alcohol
3. Get enough sleep
4. Practice breathing techniques
5. Challenge negative thoughts
6. Establish a routine
7. Engage in hobbies and activities
8. Seek social support
9. Limit exposure to triggers
10. Consider relaxation techniques
11. Practice self-compassion

Remember that managing anxiety is a process, and different strategies work for different people. It is essential to be patient with yourself and to seek professional help if you find that anxiety is significantly impacting your daily life.

(For those who can help with suicide prevention)

The essence of empathy lies in the ability to understand and share the feelings and experiences of others. It involves putting yourself in someone else's shoes, seeing the world from their perspective, and connecting with their emotions. Empathy goes beyond sympathy, which is compassion or pity for someone else's situation. Empathy is about truly understanding and relating to others, acknowledging their emotions, and responding in a compassionate and supportive manner.

There are *"Seven Pillars of Empathy"* that conjure up the essence of empathy.

Perspective taking: This is the capacity to see and understand the world from another person's point of view. It involves stepping into someone else's shoes and imagining their thoughts, feelings, and experiences.

Emotional contagion: This is the unconscious mimicry of another person's emotions. When you observe someone expressing a particular emotion, you may start to feel a similar emotion, as if it is contagious.

Empathic concern: This concern is the emotional response of caring and concern for others' well-being. It's the genuine compassion and desire to alleviate the suffering or distress of others.

Personal distress: This is the tendency to feel anxious or uncomfortable in response to witnessing the pain or suffering of others. This can lead to the avoidance of empathy because it causes discomfort.

Empathic accuracy: Empathic accuracy is the ability to accurately perceive and understand the emotions and thoughts of others. It involves correctly interpreting verbal and nonverbal cues.

Empathic responsiveness: This is responding to another person's emotional state with appropriate and empathetic reactions, such as offering support, encouragement, or comfort.

Empathic imagination: This is the capacity to imaginatively project oneself into hypothetical situations to understand how others might feel or respond in those circumstances.

It is essential to note that empathy is a complex and multifaceted construct, and these components can interact in different ways depending on the context and individuals involved. Cultivating empathy can lead to better relationships, improved communication, and a more compassionate and understanding society. Empathy is fundamental to human connection, fostering understanding, cooperation, and positive relationships. It allows us to build bridges of compassion and support, creating a more empathetic and caring culture.

Emotional resonance: Empathy involves the capacity to feel and share the emotions of others. It means being attuned to their emotional state, recognizing their joy, pain, or sadness, and connecting emotionally.

Analyse how you share and process the emotions of others.

Non-judgmental acceptance: Empathy necessitates a willingness to suspend judgment and to accept others as they are without imposing your values or expectations on them. It involves creating a safe and supportive space for people to express themselves freely.

How do you encourage others to express themselves?

Active listening: Empathy requires listening to others, not only to their words but also to their body language, tone of voice, and emotions. It involves giving your full attention, showing genuine interest, and validating your experiences.

What aspects of body language do you notice, and how do you process this information?

Compassionate response: Empathy is not just about understanding; it also involves responding with compassion and support. It means offering comfort, encouragement, and assistance to others in a way that meets their needs and respects their autonomy.

How do you encourage people and respect them at the same time?

"Change often occurs when we are ready to give up." - anonymous.

Tool 2. Building Emotional Resilience and Intelligence

(For those struggling with suicidal thoughts)

Building emotional resilience is crucial for navigating life's challenges and maintaining mental well-being. Here are some tips to help you cultivate emotional resilience:

Develop a robust support system: Surround yourself with supportive and understanding people. Having friends, family, or a support group you can lean on during tough times can significantly affect how you cope with stress.

Practice mindfulness and self-awareness: Be attuned to your emotions without judgment. Mindfulness helps you recognize and accept your feelings, allowing you to respond healthily rather than be overwhelmed by them.

Regular physical activity: Engage in regular exercise or physical activity. Physical activity can help reduce stress, release endorphins (feel-good hormones), and improve overall mood.

Learn healthy coping strategies: Avoid unhealthy coping mechanisms like excessive alcohol consumption or substance abuse. Instead, focus on constructive methods of dealing with stress, such as journaling, meditation, deep breathing exercises, or engaging in hobbies you enjoy.

Cultivate optimism: Practice seeing the positive aspects of challenging situations. Cultivating optimism does not mean denying negative emotions but reframing your thoughts to focus on potential growth and learning from difficulties.

Set realistic goals: Break down significant goals into smaller, achievable steps. This approach helps prevent feeling overwhelmed and gives you a sense of accomplishment as you progress.

Embrace change: Life is full of changes and being adaptable can increase your emotional resilience. Embrace change as an opportunity for growth and learning rather than viewing it as a threat.

Practice self-compassion: Be kind to yourself during difficult times. Treat yourself with the same level of compassion and understanding that you would offer to a friend facing a challenge.

Develop problem-solving skills: Work on developing effective problem-solving skills to address challenges proactively. Analyse the situation, explore potential solutions, and take action.

Limit exposure to negativity: Be mindful of the media you consume and the people you interact with. Limit exposure to negative influences that could heighten stress and anxiety.

Seek professional help if needed: If you find it challenging to cope with your emotions or if you are dealing with a complicated situation, do not hesitate to seek support from a mental health professional.

Cultivate gratitude: Practice gratitude regularly by acknowledging and appreciating the positive aspects of your life. This practice can help shift your focus from negativity to a positive outlook.

Remember that building emotional resilience takes time and effort. It is okay to experience setbacks or emotional challenges along the way. What matters most is your commitment to improving your resilience and willingness to seek support when needed.

(For those who can help with suicide prevention)

Building emotional intelligence is a valuable skill that can help you navigate social interactions, manage your own emotions, and understand the feelings of others. Here are some tips to develop and improve your emotional intelligence:

Self-awareness: Pay attention to your emotions and the triggers that lead to specific feelings. Be honest with yourself about your emotional state, strengths, and areas for improvement.

Active listening: Pay attention when others speak without interrupting or thinking about what you will say next. Validate their feelings and show genuine interest in their experiences.

Emotional regulation: Learn to manage your emotions effectively. Instead of reacting impulsively, take a moment to reflect on your feelings and choose a thoughtful response.

Social skills: Develop strong communication skills and learn to express your emotions clearly and respectfully—also, practice constructively resolving conflicts.

Recognize non-verbal cues: Observe and interpret body language, facial expressions, and tone of voice to understand the emotions behind someone's words.

Practice empathy: Put yourself in others' shoes to better understand their feelings and motivations. This will help you connect with them on a deeper level.

Reflect on your emotions: Regularly reflect on your emotional reactions and consider how you could have handled situations differently.

Learn from feedback: Be open to feedback from others about your emotional responses and communication style. Use constructive criticism to improve your emotional intelligence.

Develop resilience: Emotional intelligence involves returning from setbacks and learning from challenges. Build resilience by developing coping strategies for stress and adversity.

Cultivate positive relationships: Nurture your relationships with friends, family, and colleagues by being supportive, understanding, and empathetic.

Read emotional cues in others: Observe and understand the emotions of people around you. This will help you respond appropriately to their needs.

Practice patience: Building emotional intelligence takes time and effort. Be patient with yourself as you develop these skills.

Seek professional help if needed: If you find it challenging to manage your emotions or connect with others, consider seeking guidance from a therapist or counsellor who can provide personalized support.

Remember that emotional intelligence is an ongoing journey, and it is expected to encounter setbacks along the way. Stay committed to your growth and practice these tips regularly to enhance your emotional intelligence over time.

Identify all the inaccurate assumptions you are making right now or that you have made in the past.

Accessing your intuition is the key to unlocking your future.

Raw ingredients = ambition + desire + love + zeal + tenacity + goals + curiosity + vision

"The secret to change is to focus all of your energy not on fighting the old but on building the new." - Socrates.

Tool 3. Living YOUR Mission

(For those struggling with suicidal thoughts)

In life's journey, each of us is bestowed with a unique purpose, a mission intricately woven into the fabric of our being. It is the reason we exist, the driving force behind our thoughts, actions, and aspirations. Living your mission is a profound and transformative experience that can elevate your life to new heights, allowing you to leave a lasting impact on the world and find true fulfilment.

Discovering your mission: Living your mission begins with self-discovery. Take a moment to reflect on your passions, values, and strengths. What activities make you lose track of time? What issues ignite a fire within you? Embrace your uniqueness and recognize that no one else can fulfil your mission as well as you can. Trust that the universe has a purpose for you, and your journey is essential to a more remarkable tapestry.

Believe in yourself: The path to fulfilling your mission may be riddled with challenges and doubts. There will be moments when the world questions your abilities, and even you may question yourself. Embrace these moments of uncertainty as opportunities for growth. Remember that greatness is not achieved by those who never stumble but by those who rise each time they fall. Believe in your innate abilities, and let your unwavering faith guide you through dark times.

Set clear intentions: To live your mission with purpose, set clear intentions. Define what success looks like to you personally and in your mission's context. What impact do you wish to create? How will it enrich not only your life but the lives of others? Allow these intentions to become your compass, leading you towards your purpose with unwavering dedication.

Embrace challenges as steppingstones: Obstacles are an inevitable part of any meaningful journey. Embrace them as steppingstones rather than roadblocks. Each challenge presents an opportunity to learn, grow, and refine your purpose. Remember that setbacks do not define you; your response genuinely matters. Approach challenges with resilience and let them strengthen your determination to live your mission.

Stay true to your values: In pursuing your mission, you might encounter temptations to compromise your values or take shortcuts. Resist such temptations with unyielding resolve. Your mission's authenticity lies in staying true to your principles, even when it seems complicated. When you align your actions with your values, you create a powerful impact that resonates far beyond your immediate sphere of influence.

Cultivate perseverance: Living your mission is not a sprint; it is a marathon. Cultivate perseverance, for true success rarely comes overnight. Be patient with yourself and the process. Celebrate every small victory and use setbacks as opportunities to learn and grow. As you persevere, you build the resilience to surmount any obstacles and manifest your mission in full splendour.

Empower others: Your mission is not solely about personal accomplishment; it is about creating a ripple effect of positive change in the lives of others. Inspire and empower those around you to also discover and live their missions. Remember that we are all interconnected, and the collective fulfilment of missions can bring about profound transformations in the world.

Celebrate the journey: Amidst the pursuit of your mission, do not forget to cherish the journey itself. Every step, every experience, and every encounter have the potential to enrich your life. Find joy in the process and savour the growth it brings. Celebrate the person you become in the pursuit of your mission, for it is this growth that makes your purpose so profound.

Living your mission is an extraordinary gift - a testament to the human spirit's power to dream, dare, and achieve. As you embark on this sacred journey, remember that the world eagerly awaits the expression of your purpose. Embrace it with open arms and let the light of your mission illuminate the world around you.

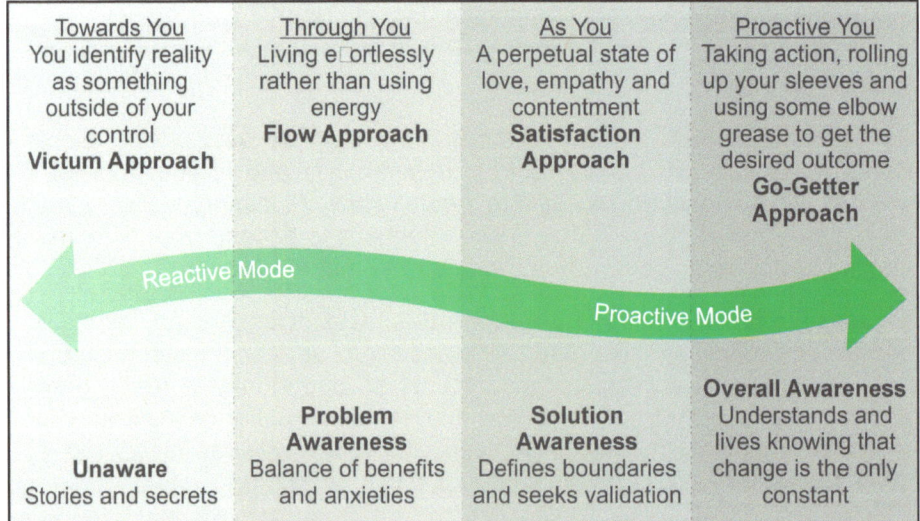

Image 13: Stages of Awareness

(For those who can help with suicide prevention)

Inclusion is more than a buzzword. It scratches beyond the surface. It touches the heart of the matter, which is not merely about existing but thriving. It is about accepting the whole person and their differences. The way they manage their lives, their entire person with their limitations. Inclusion makes room and space instead of leaving others to feel more isolated and emptier. Ask the critical questions and follow up with action:

1. Could you help me understand the situation?
2. How can I support you?
3. How can I make a difference?

Many people are left out. In employment situations. In community circles. In conversations. Even at Houses of Worship and, sadly, also in families. Imagine the circle expanding for others, creating space for everyone, and opening our arms. Hearts. For those already included, you truly cannot fathom the opposite. However, denial does not eradicate reality. We can all do better.

Create a list of how you will proactively include people.

"One of the most cowardly things that people do is to shut their eyes to the facts." - C.S. Lewis.

Tool 4. Anxiety Versus Stress

In the movie *"Forrest Gump,"* there is a touching scene where Forrest meets Jenny by a river, and they have a heart-to-heart conversation. Jenny is going through a difficult time, and Forrest is trying to comfort her. They arrive at the house that Jenny grew up in. Jenny begins to cry, then picks up a rock and throws it at the house. She feels a sense of release and grabs another rock, then another. After she lets out her steam, Forrest says, *"Sometimes there just isn't enough rocks."* In life, we are often presented with heart-warming moments of restoration born out of despair. Allow these poignant moments to resonate with you and help you find your balance. Fear and anxiety are related but distinct emotional experiences. They both involve a sense of unease but differ in their triggers, intensity, and nature.

Fear:

Trigger: Fear is a natural response to a specific, identifiable threat or danger. It arises when we encounter a real and immediate threat, such as facing a dangerous animal, being in a life-threatening situation, or experiencing a sudden and alarming event.

Intensity: Fear tends to be intense and acute, causing a "fight or flight" response. This response prepares the body to react quickly to the perceived threat by confronting it or escaping it.

Focus: Fear is often focused on the present or immediate future and is closely tied to the specific trigger or situation that elicits it.

Duration: Fear typically subsides once the threat has passed or when the individual is no longer exposed to the triggering situation.

Anxiety:

Trigger: Anxiety, on the other hand, is a more generalized and prolonged emotional response. It may not always have a specific or identifiable trigger and can be related to various sources of uncertainty, potential future threats, or worries.

Intensity: Anxiety can range from mild to severe, and unlike fear, it is not necessarily associated with an imminent threat or danger.

Focus: Anxiety often involves a broad range of concerns and may not be linked to a particular event or situation. It can be related to various aspects of life, such as health, relationships, work, or personal issues.

Duration: Anxiety can be chronic and persist over an extended period, lasting days, weeks, or even months, depending on the underlying causes and coping mechanisms of the individual. Fear is a response to an immediate and identifiable threat, while anxiety is a more general and prolonged emotional state related to potential threats and uncertainties.

Both emotions are typical human experiences, but excessive or persistent fear and anxiety can be problematic and may require attention and support to manage them effectively. Fear is a polarised emotion that results from an assumption that you are about to experience in the immediate or distant future, through your sensors or imagination, more loss than gain, more negatives than positives, more pain than pleasure, more disadvantages than advantages, and more risk than rewards. As you neutralise your emotions and go into this more balanced and reasonable state, you will likely get to a point where you do not fear loss or gain. Perhaps you are not healing because you are trying to be who you were before the trauma. Realise that person does not exist because you have merged from the cocoon of pain. You need to breathe life into that new person. You are more powerful than any damage inflicted on you, and you will rise from any abyss that tries to drown you. Always remember not to live life according to what people dish out, but by the answer, you serve yourself.

Restrictions and hard-hitting imperfections do not characterise you. The true you - a robust, remarkable human - is revealed when you tap into your resilience and become a warrior.

Only you can paint your story, and you are the finest at telling your story. Your story is unique, and it originates from your heart. With all the setbacks, portray your life as a tenacious conqueror. Life is not made up of one single ingredient. It is a rich, multifaceted layer: love comes with loss. Guaranteed with birth, grief follows. Promised courage will be coupled with vulnerability. Indeed, power and humility will struggle. Perfectionism has never been prescribed to anyone. Life is a hustle; you must get up each morning and propel yourself. The highest currency in the world is love. Let it begin with loving yourself. Never give up on yourself. Everyone has gone through something that has profoundly changed them, and they could never return to being the person they used to be.

List all your fears and anxiety, then ask someone to help you address them. Re-evaluate how you feel after three months with each situation:

1. Better than I expected
2. Just as I expected
3. Worse than I had expected

"The secret of change is to focus all of your energy not on fighting the old but on building the new." - Socrates.

Tool 5. The Optimism Gallery

Pain is inevitable. Suffering is optional.

Other people liking you is a bonus. You liking yourself is the real prize.

Instead of trying to toughen up and develop a thicker skin, create healthy boundaries honouring soft courage and compassion.

Push yourself harder than yesterday if you want a different tomorrow.

Misery may love company, and so does joy. Remember, joy throws a much better party.

Sometimes, you must take a moment to pause and remind yourself that even though life has not been perfect, there is so much to be grateful for.

If you ever feel like you are falling apart and want to cry for no reason, reach out to someone who will sit with you and cry until you both begin to laugh.

If you stay silent about the problem to keep the peace, there is a low possibility that you will find a solution.

There are two places you need to go to often: one that heals you and one that inspires you.

The season of loneliness and isolation happens when the caterpillar gets its wings. Remember that the next time you feel alone.

Never fake it until you make it. Face it until you make it. Get back on the horse. Work hard. Fail. Dust yourself. Take time out. Try again. Take a rest if you need to. Have another try and do it a little bit better. Fail again. Try again. It is better to try and fail rather than fail to try. FAILED - try again and again.

You have a clean slate daily; wake up each morning and change the narrative.

Always remember that you are valuable because you exist, not because of your limitations, status, or anything else, but simply because of who you are.

Nothing great is ever achieved without endurance.

Last week, you may have found yourself frazzled. You may be under divine pressure this week because you are bearing something profound. A narrative shift is a reality to be reckoned with. Courage begins with the little steps. One day, you may meet someone who cares not for status, money, or position, and then you will realise how far you are. Fix your focus on eternal assets that confirm it is well with your soul.

Stop blaming and resenting people for showing up in ways that do not align with you. If you allow people who do not align with your values, your growth may be hindered. Introspect and enhance your circle.

Some people will judge you for changing. Others will celebrate your development. Choose your circle wisely.

Tough times never last as long as durable people do.

Your progress does not need to be seen by or validated by others.

Be the designer of your own life.

Do not hold onto resentment if it costs you the ultimate price.

Not every provocation is meant to shatter you; some triggers are essential to mend you if you allow them.

Unforgiveness is the only prison with locks on the inside.

When in doubt, choose joy.

God does not disqualify you, so never disqualify yourself.

Pandora also found hope at the bottom of her box, so take comfort.

Shame dies, and stories are told in a safe place. Find your safe place.

If you are walking in the valley, you do not have to journey by yourself. Talk to someone. Lay down your burdens.

Do not forget that you also get thirsty; never be afraid to let someone quench you.

Sometimes, the future comes from unexpected directions.

Be informed by the simple and eloquent command to love one another, even if they have wronged you.

Family may not be your blood in attitude. Because the soul has a different path from the body, cut them loose if they hinder your welfare.

Your piece is worth more than proving yourself to anyone.

Never sit around looking like an envelope without an address and stamp on it. Get up and go places, even at a snail's pace.

As difficult as it may be, you have to reach a point where you must leave the burdens of your experience behind and share the beauty of the lessons.

Peace gushes when you remember it is not up to you to always figure everything out.

Some mornings, you must remind yourself that you got through yesterday and will undoubtedly get through today.

Sweet friendship refreshes the soul. Appreciate those in your circle who provide wise, faithful counsel and have your best interests at heart, especially when struggling to cope. Celebrate with these gems.

As soon as you figure out who does not belong at your table, your meals will become more peaceful.

Perfectionism is not just a trait; it is a silent killer that can drain our energy and steal precious moments of joy from our lives. Perfectionism was merely a mask for inner insecurities and the fear of failure. Embracing imperfection allows you to work more from intuition and confidence rather than being clouded by insecurity and fear.

Growth happens when you step out of your comfort zone, allowing yourself to stumble, learn, and rise stronger than before.

Sometimes, it is the help that you will never get that will help you the most.

Sunshine always follows the rain.

Life constantly changes. You lose people. You discover the real abundance of a person's heart. You may lose pieces of yourself that you never imagined would be gone. This is the crux of life. Keep going and focus on the destination rather than the journey.

Image 14: Self-Love Affirmations

1. Embrace your uniqueness, your strengths, and your quirks, for that is what makes you extraordinary.
2. Life has no checklist on tape. You create your own rules - a significant feat for life.

"Great spirits have always encountered violent opposition from mediocre minds." - Albert Einstein.

Tool 6. Mandatory Reporting

Why People May Not Report Suicide

There are several reasons why people may not report or talk about suicide, and it is essential to understand these factors to address the issue effectively. Here are some common reasons:

Stigma: There is a significant social stigma surrounding suicide and mental health issues in many societies. People may fear being judged, labelled as weak or unstable, or facing discrimination if they reveal their struggles or thoughts about suicide.

Shame and guilt: Individuals experiencing suicidal thoughts or those close to someone who died by suicide may feel ashamed or guilty about their emotions or their inability to prevent the situation.

Fear of consequences: Some individuals might fear the consequences of seeking help, such as being involuntarily hospitalized, losing their jobs, or being alienated from friends and family.

Lack of understanding: Many people may not fully understand the signs and risk factors associated with suicide, leading them to dismiss or overlook concerning behaviours.

Lack of support: People may fear that others would not take them seriously or would not be supportive if they disclosed their suicidal thoughts or feelings.

Isolation: Those struggling with suicidal thoughts may feel isolated and believe that no one will understand what they are going through.

Minimizing or denying the problem: Some individuals may downplay their emotional distress, making it difficult for others to recognize the seriousness of the situation.

Cultural or religious beliefs: Cultural or religious beliefs may discourage open discussions about mental health or suicide, leading people to keep their feelings and struggles to themselves.

Communication barriers: Language, communication style, and cultural differences can hinder individuals from effectively expressing their emotions or seeking help.

Lack of resources: In some regions, mental health services may be limited, inaccessible, or stigmatized, making it challenging for individuals to find appropriate support.

It is crucial to break down these barriers and encourage open conversations about human welfare and suicide. Building a supportive and understanding community can help individuals feel more comfortable seeking help when needed. If you or someone you know is experiencing thoughts of suicide, it is essential to reach out to a mental health professional or a helpline immediately. Remember that talking about suicide with compassion and without judgment can save lives.

How to Generate Mandatory Reports

Creating mandatory reporting for suicide statistics involves several steps to ensure accurate and timely reporting while maintaining sensitivity to the topic. Below is a suggested workflow:

Step 1. Define reporting parameters: Establish clear definitions for what constitutes a suicide case that needs to be reported. This ensures consistency in conveying across different sources and jurisdictions.

Step 2. Identify reporting entities: Determine the entities responsible for reporting suicide statistics. This could include healthcare facilities, law enforcement agencies, mental health professionals, schools, crisis hotlines, etc.

Step 3. Training and awareness: Provide training to the reporting entities on recognizing, documenting, and reporting suicide cases. This training should include guidance on handling sensitive information and maintaining confidentiality.

Step 4. Data collection: Reporting entities should collect relevant information about each suicide case, such as demographic details, circumstances, and any available mental health history. Use standardized forms to ensure consistency.

Step 5. Data aggregation: Establish a centralized reporting system or database where collected data can be aggregated. This could be a government agency, a mental health organization, or another appropriate entity.

Step 6. Data Analysis: Regularly analyse the aggregated data to identify trends, risk factors, and potential interventions. This can aid in developing targeted prevention strategies.

Step 7. Reporting schedule: Set up a reporting schedule outlining when and how often data needs to be submitted to the centralized system. This could be monthly, quarterly, or annually.

Step 8. Data verification: Implement a verification process to ensure the accuracy of the reported data. This might involve cross-referencing data with other sources or conducting audits.

Step 9. Privacy and confidentiality: Emphasize the importance of protecting the privacy and confidentiality of individuals involved. Follow appropriate data protection laws and ethical guidelines.

Step 10. Reporting format: Create a standardized reporting format that includes vital statistics, such as the number of suicides, demographics, methods used, and any notable trends.

Step 11. Reporting channels: Specify the channels through which reporting entities should submit their data. This could include online portals, secure email, or direct data transfers.

Step 12. Data sharing and communication: Establish guidelines for sharing the aggregated data with relevant stakeholders, such as government agencies, mental health organizations, researchers, and the public. Ensure the data is presented responsibly to avoid sensationalism.

Step 13. Continuous improvement: Regularly assess the reporting workflow for effectiveness and make improvements as needed. This could involve seeking feedback from reporting entities, analysing the challenges, and updating protocols accordingly.

Step 14. Legal and ethical considerations: Ensure the reporting workflow adheres to legal requirements, including reporting mandates or data protection regulations. Additionally, it addresses ethical considerations related to reporting sensitive information.

By following these steps, you can create a comprehensive mandatory reporting workflow for suicide statistics that balances the need for accurate data with sensitivity to the individuals and communities affected by this serious issue.

How to Report Suicide

Reporting suicide statistics requires sensitivity and responsible communication to avoid potential harm and to adhere to ethical guidelines. Mandatory reporting is a legislative requirement for cases of suicide in certain countries; this helps facilitate reform. Here are some steps to consider when reporting suicide statistics:

Verify the data: Ensure that the statistics you report are from reputable sources such as government health departments, recognized research institutions, or reputable non-profit organizations. Verify the accuracy and validity of the data to avoid spreading misinformation.

Use appropriate language: Use neutral and non-sensational language when reporting suicide statistics. Avoid using terms that glamorize or romanticize suicide, as they can be harmful to vulnerable individuals.

Provide context: Put the statistics in context by explaining what they represent and how they were gathered. For example, include information about the time frame, geographical area, and demographics.

Avoid graphic details: Do not include graphic details or methods of suicide in your report. This information can be distressing to readers and may inadvertently contribute to copycat behaviour.

Include prevention resources: When reporting on suicide statistics, include information about suicide prevention resources such as hotlines, support organizations, and websites. Encouraging help-seeking behaviour is essential.

Discuss risk factors and warning signs: Alongside the statistics, provide information about common risk factors and warning signs of suicide. Raising awareness about these factors can help readers identify when someone might be distressed and need support.

Avoid speculation: Stick to the available data and avoid speculating on the reasons behind the statistics. Speculation can lead to misunderstandings and misinterpretations.

Be cautious with headlines: Craft factual, sensitive, and accurate headlines. Avoid sensationalizing suicide or using phrases that could trigger vulnerable individuals.

Seek expert input: If possible, consult with mental health experts or suicide prevention organizations when reporting on suicide statistics. They can offer valuable insights and guidance on handling the topic responsibly.

Monitor comments and feedback: If your report is published online, keep an eye on comments and feedback. Respond appropriately to potentially harmful or triggering comments and consider moderating discussions to maintain a safe environment.

Remember that responsible reporting on suicide statistics can play a role in raising awareness, reducing stigma, and promoting human welfare. Be mindful of the potential impact of your words, and always prioritize the safety and well-being of your audience.

When to Take Crucial, Immediate Action

If you suspect someone might be at risk of suicide, it is crucial to take immediate action. Here is a general guideline on how to handle reporting a potential suicide:

Assess the situation: If you are concerned about someone's well-being and suspect they might be contemplating suicide, it is essential to take their situation seriously. Look for warning signs like talking about suicide, giving away possessions, withdrawing from friends and family, or displaying sudden changes in behaviour.

Stay calm and supportive: If the person is willing to talk, lend a listening ear without judgment. Let them know that you care and are there to support them.

Direct communication: If you feel comfortable, ask them directly if they are thinking about suicide. This can open up a conversation about their feelings and intentions.

Do not leave them alone: If you believe the person is an immediate danger to themselves, do not leave them alone. Try to keep them engaged in conversation and seek help.

Contact a mental health professional: If the person is open to it, help them contact a mental health professional or counsellor who can provide immediate support. This could be a therapist, psychiatrist, or counsellor.

Contact emergency services: If the person is in imminent danger and you fear for their safety, do not hesitate to call emergency services (911 or your local emergency number) and let them know about the situation.

Contact friends or family: Reach out to their close friends or family members, who can also provide support and assistance.

National hotlines: If you are unsure how to proceed, you can also contact a suicide prevention hotline in your country. They have trained professionals who can provide guidance and support. Some examples include the National Suicide Prevention Lifeline (1-800-273-TALK) in the United States.

Document the situation: If you have been in communication with the person, make sure to document what they have said and any actions you have taken. This information might be helpful for mental health professionals who become involved later.

Remember, your role is to provide support and help connect the person to appropriate resources. It is important to involve professionals trained to handle such situations, as suicide is a complex issue. If you ever feel that someone's life is in immediate danger, do not hesitate to call emergency services.

"You are today where your thoughts have brought you; you will be tomorrow where your thoughts take you." - James Allen.

Tool 7. The Dos and Don'ts of Suicide

How to support someone who is grieving: The bereaved struggles with many intense and painful emotions, including depression, anger, guilt, and profound sadness. Often, they also feel isolated and alone in their grief since the intense pain and complicated emotions can make people uncomfortable about offering support. Never let discomfort prevent you from reaching out to someone who is grieving. Now, more than ever, your loved one needs your support. You do not need to have answers, give advice, or say and do all the right things. The most important thing you can do for a grieving person is to simply be there. Your support and caring presence will help your loved one cope with the pain and gradually begin to heal.

The keys to helping a grieving loved one: Do not let fears about saying or doing the wrong thing stop you from reaching out. Let your grieving loved one know that you are there to listen. Understand that everyone grieves differently and for different lengths of time. Offer to help in practical ways.

Understand the grieving process: There is no right or wrong way to grieve. Grief does not always unfold in orderly, predictable stages. It can be an emotional rollercoaster, with unpredictable highs, lows, and setbacks. Everyone grieves differently, so avoid telling your loved one what they *"should"* feel or do. Grief may involve extreme emotions and behaviours. Feelings of guilt, anger, despair, and fear are common. A grieving person may yell to the heavens, obsess about death, lash out at loved ones, or cry for hours on end. Your loved one needs reassurance that what they feel is normal. Do not judge them or take their grief reactions personally. There is no set timetable for grieving. For many people, recovery after bereavement takes 18 to 24 months, but for others, the grieving process may be longer or shorter. Do not pressure your loved one to move on or make them feel like they have been grieving too long. This can slow down the healing process.

Know what to say to someone who is grieving: While many of us worry about what to say to a grieving person, it is more important to listen. Oftentimes, well-meaning people avoid talking about the death or change the subject when the deceased person is mentioned. Or, knowing there is nothing they can say to make it better, they try to avoid the grieving person altogether. However, the bereaved need to feel that their loss is acknowledged, it is not too terrible to talk about, and their loved one will not be forgotten.

How to talk to and listen to someone grieving: While you should never force someone to open up, it is essential to let your grieving friend or loved one know you are there to listen if they want to talk about their loss. Talk candidly about the person who died, and do not steer away from the subject if the deceased's name comes up. And when it seems appropriate, ask sensitive questions - without being nosy - that invite the grieving person to express their feelings openly. By simply asking, "Do you feel like talking?" you are letting your loved one know you are available to listen.

Acknowledge the situation: For example, you could say something as simple as: *"I heard that your father died."* By using the word *"died,"* you will show that you are more open to talking about how the grieving person feels.

Express your concern: For example, say, *"I'm sorry to hear that this happened to you."* Let the bereaved talk about how their loved one died. People who are grieving may need to tell the story over and over again, sometimes in minute detail. Be patient. Repeating the story is a way of processing and accepting the death. With each retelling, the pain lessens. By listening patiently and compassionately, you are helping your loved one heal.

Ask how your loved one feels: The emotions of grief can change rapidly, so do not assume you know how the bereaved person feels at any given time. If you have gone through a similar loss, share your experience if you think it would help. Remember, though, that grief is an intensely individual experience. No two people experience it the same way, so do not claim to *"know"* what the other person is feeling or compare your grief to theirs.

Accept your loved one's feelings: Let the grieving person know that it is okay to cry in front of you, to get angry, or to break down. Do not try to reason with them over how they should or should not feel. Grief is a highly emotional experience, so the bereaved need to feel free to express their feelings - no matter how irrational - without fear of judgement, argument, or criticism.

Be genuine in your communication: Do not try to minimize their loss, provide simplistic solutions, or offer unsolicited advice. It is far better to listen to your loved one or simply admit, *"I'm not sure what to say, but I want you to know I care."*

Be willing to sit in silence: Do not press if the grieving person does not feel like talking. Often, comfort for them comes from simply being in your company. If you cannot think of something to say, offer eye contact, a hand squeeze, or a reassuring hug.

Offer your support: Ask what you can do for the grieving person. Offer to help with a specific task, such as helping with funeral arrangements, being there to hang out with, or as a shoulder to cry on.

Things to avoid saying to someone grieving: *"It's part of God's plan."* This platitude can anger people. Often, they will respond with, *"What plan? Nobody* *told me about any plan." "Look at what you have to be thankful for."* They know they have things to be thankful for, but they are not important right now. *"He's in a better place now."* The bereaved may or may not believe this. Keep your beliefs to yourself unless asked. *"This is behind you now; it's time to get on with your life."* Sometimes, the bereaved are resistant to getting on it because they feel this means "forgetting" their loved one. Besides, moving on is much easier said than done. Grief has a mind of its own and works at its own pace. Statements that begin with *"You should"* or *"You will"* are too directive. Instead, you could start your comments with, *"Have you thought about…"* or *"You might try…"*

Offer practical assistance: It is difficult for many grieving people to ask for help. They might feel guilty about receiving so much attention, fear being a burden to others, or be too depressed to reach out. A grieving person may not have the energy or motivation to call you when they need something, so instead of saying, *"Let me know if there's anything I can do,"* make it easier for them by making specific suggestions. You could say, *"I'm going to the market this afternoon. What can I bring you from there?"* or, *"I've made beef stew for dinner. When can I come by and bring you some?"*

Provide ongoing support: Your loved one will continue grieving long after the funeral is over and the cards and flowers have stopped. The length of the grieving process varies from person to person but often lasts much longer than most people expect. Your bereaved friend or family member may need your support for months or years. Continue your support over the long haul. Stay in touch with the grieving person, periodically checking in, dropping by, or sending letters or cards. Once the funeral is over, the other mourners are gone, and the initial shock of the loss has worn off, your support is more valuable than ever.

Do not make assumptions based on outward appearances: The bereaved person may look fine on the outside, but inside, they are suffering. Avoid saying things like, *"You are so strong,"* or, *"You look so well."* This pressures the person to keep up appearances and hide their true feelings. The pain of grief may never fully heal. Be sensitive to the fact that life may never feel the same. You do not *"get over"* the death of a loved one. The bereaved person may learn to accept the loss. The pain may intensify over time, but the sadness may never completely disappear.

Offer extra support on special days: Certain times and days of the year will be tough for your grieving friend or family member. Holidays, family milestones, birthdays, and anniversaries often reawaken grief. Be sensitive on these occasions. Let the bereaved person know that you are there for whatever they need.

Watch for warning signs of depression: It is common for a grieving person to feel depressed, confused, disconnected from others, or like they are going crazy. But if the bereaved person's symptoms do not gradually start to fade—or get worse with time—this may be a sign that normal grief has evolved into a more serious problem, such as clinical depression. Encourage the grieving person to seek professional help if you observe any of the following warning signs after the initial grieving period—especially if it has been over two months since the death. Watch for these signs:

- Difficulty functioning in daily life
- Extreme focus on the death
- Excessive bitterness, anger, or guilt
- Neglecting personal hygiene
- Alcohol or drug abuse
- Inability to enjoy life
- Hallucinations
- Withdrawing from others
- Constant feelings of hopelessness
- Talking about dying or suicide

"I count him braver who overcomes his desires than him who conquers his enemies, for the hardest victory is over self." - Aristotle.

Tool 8. Risk Assessment

Vital Information when assessing risks and issues

Please note that this information is not a substitute for professional guidance, especially in cases involving sensitive issues like suicide. If you are dealing with a specific situation, it is important to involve mental health professionals or experts who can provide appropriate assistance.

Understanding risk assessment

Risk assessment is used to identify potential risks in a service or situation in a systematic way and provide an opportunity to identify activities and the risks these can pose separately. This systematic process allows a more objective assessment of services, situations, and activities. An intuitive approach can vary from person to person. Understand that this is not one size that will fit all.

Risks

Risk management is the ability to identify what might go wrong. These are the adverse risks, otherwise known as threats. It is crucial to identify and record them in your risk register to understand what might be coming around the corner to interfere with your chances of success. But identifying them is only the beginning. Once you have done that, you must also determine what to do about them.

Risk Register

Rating	Risks	Risk Owner	Consequence	Likelihood	Mitigation Plan
R1	Someone informs you that they are considering suicide	**Recipient**	Catastrophic	Almost certain	**Assess, evaluate and develop a plan.** **It is critical to monitor and follow up**
R2	Someone texts you about ending their life and sends you a picture of a noose.	**Recipient**	Catastrophic	Almost certain	**Assess, evaluate and develop a plan.** **It is critical to monitor and follow up**

The basic framework for conducting a risk assessment:

Gather Information: Obtain relevant information about the individual's situation, mental health history, and any recent changes in behaviour or circumstances. This may involve talking to the individual directly or consulting with family, friends, or other support networks.

Identify risk factors: Recognize the factors that contribute to an increased risk of suicide. These can include, but are not limited to:

- History of previous suicide attempts
- Mental health disorders (e.g., depression, bipolar disorder)
- Substance abuse
- Recent loss or trauma
- Social isolation
- Access to lethal means
- Family history of suicide
- Lack of social support

- Chronic pain or illness
- Victim of any form of abuse - Financial, emotional, or physical

Assess protective factors: Consider the factors that may help reduce the individual's risk of suicide. These can include:

- Strong social support system
- Access to mental health care
- Positive coping skills
- Religious or cultural beliefs that discourage suicide
- Sense of responsibility to loved ones

Evaluate warning signs: Look for signs indicating immediate risk or heightened concern. These may include:

- Talking about suicide, death, or a desire to die
- Expressing feelings of hopelessness or worthlessness
- Giving away belongings
- Sudden withdrawal from social activities
- Drastic changes in behaviour or mood

Determine severity: Assess the severity of the individual's risk. This could involve using a standardized assessment tool or clinical judgement to categorize the risk as low, moderate, or high.

Develop a safety plan: Collaborate with the individual to create a safety plan outlining steps to manage their distress and stay safe. This may involve identifying coping strategies, supportive contacts, and emergency resources.

Provide support and referrals: Offer immediate support and connect the individual to appropriate mental health services. Ensure they can access help and encourage them to engage in ongoing treatment.

Monitor and follow up: Regularly check in with the individual to assess their progress, adherence to the safety plan, and any changes in their condition. Follow up with mental health professionals, as necessary.

Remember, this outline is a general guide and should be adapted to everyone's unique circumstances. If you are dealing with a potentially high-risk situation, it is crucial to involve mental health professionals, crisis hotlines, or emergency services.

Risk Rating Matrix

A risk rating matrix is a graphical tool used to assess and prioritize risks based on their likelihood and potential impact. It provides a visual representation of different risk scenarios and helps make informed decisions about managing and mitigating these risks. The risk matrix typically consists of a grid or table with likelihood on one axis and impact on the other axis, and different risk levels are assigned different colours. You can assign risk ratings based on the intersection of the likelihood and consequence categories. These ratings help prioritize risks and determine the appropriate response strategies.

		Consequence				
		Insignificant	Minor	Moderate	Major	Disastrous
Certainty Level	Almost Certain	Moderate	High	High	Disastrous	Disastrous
	Likely	Moderate	Moderate	High	Disastrous	Disastrous
	Possible	Low	Moderate	Moderate	High	High
	Unlikely	Low	Moderate	Moderate	Moderate	High
	Rare	Low	Low	Low	Moderate	Moderate

Image 15: Risk Rating Matrix

"The greatest revolution of your generation is the discovery that human beings, by changing the inner attitudes of their minds, can change the outer aspects of their lives." - William James.

Tool 9. Stop, Start and Continue Matrix

The *"Stop, Start, and Continue"* (SSC) matrix is a simple and effective tool used in various contexts, such as life retrospectives and personal development, to assess and improve processes, behaviours, or strategies. The SSC matrix aims to facilitate open and constructive feedback and promote continuous improvement. It helps individuals or communities identify actions they should stop, start, or continue doing.

Here is how the SSC matrix works:

Stop: In this section, participants list actions, behaviours, or processes that they believe are counterproductive or do not bring the desired outcomes. These activities could waste time, create inefficiencies, or hinder progress.

Start: In this section, participants suggest new actions, behaviours, or processes that they believe will be beneficial and contribute positively to the team or project. These could be new ideas, approaches, or changes that can improve the current situation.

Continue: In this section, participants identify actions, behaviours, or processes currently working well and bringing positive results. These are the aspects that should be maintained and sustained going forward.

The matrix can be presented in a simple table format with three columns representing "Stop," "Start," and "Continue." Participants can contribute their ideas during a team meeting or retrospective by writing down items in the three categories.

The SSC matrix is a valuable tool because it encourages a balanced perspective. It acknowledges both the positive aspects that should be maintained and the negative aspects that need improvement. It also fosters a sense of ownership and collective responsibility within the community or individual for making necessary changes and driving progress.

Overall, the SSC matrix helps teams and individuals to self-assess, prioritize improvements, and take actionable steps towards continuous enhancement and growth.

Image 16: Stop, start, and continue

Stop

1. Stop telling people that their loved one is in a better place.
2. Stop saying it is their time to die.
3. Stop telling people this is their destiny.
4. Stop using the expression, "he committed suicide." It creates a stigma as if a loved one committed a crime. It may sound harsh, but it is easier for loved ones to process, "he killed himself."

Start

1. Responses to suicide and grief are not cold and impersonal. You must realise and understand that certain situations require more sensitive rhetoric and perspective. Every situation is different, and it should be customised. There is no one-size-fits-all approach, even when it may be a similar situation.
2. Take people seriously when they inform you that they are contemplating suicide.

Continue

1. Offer support and guidance even when you think a person is fine
2. Develop a proactive approach to human welfare

Create your stop, start, and continue matrix. Since you have now read this book on suicide, how will you improve yourself, the community, and the landscape to champion the course of suicide prevention?

"In reality, all men are sculptures, constantly chipping away the unwanted parts of their lives trying to create a masterpiece." - Eddie Murphy.

Tool 10. Prayer Pathway

People know your name, not your story. They have heard what you have done but not what you have been through. Take your opinions with a grain of salt. What matters is what God thinks of you, not what others think of you. Take your burdens to Him. Uncovering the true you means letting go of all that the world has told you to be. Go on a journey with God to reveal who you are. Never be depressed if someone refuses to help you. Quit being despondent if someone ignores you. Always remember Einstein's words: ***"I am thankful to all those who said no. Because of them, I did it myself."*** If it is too much to endure, run to God. Refrain from wasting your time on people who treat you well one day, then act like you do not exist the next day. You are not a paper plate; you are Royal Dalton. Never get caught in people pleasing you; choose the truth that you will only value what God thinks of you.

Pray that God removes everyone from your life who secretly gossips about you, puts you down, and does not want to see you win and replaces them with people who generally support you and want to see you happy and blessed. May those that dim your light be removed and replaced by a loving tribe or fuel your fire and light up your part for you. On your darkest days, when you feel inadequate, unloved, and unworthy, remember whose daughter or son you are and straighten up your crown. Here are some quick prayers that you can use at any time:

1. Lord, remove any laziness or procrastination from my mind and my body. Push me to broaden my full potential.

2. Dear God, please bring peace to my confusion, joy to my sadness, and hope to my heart.

3. King Jesus, if it is not for me, remove it. If they are not for me, reveal them.

4. Father, protect my path and never let me quit on Your will

5. Abba Father, please heal my heart and mind and remove my worries.

Affirm these affirmations and learn the Scriptures to speak to them over your life when needed.

"The Lord is my Shepherd, I shall not want though I walk through the valley of the shadow of death, I will fear no evil for thou art with me, they road and they staff they comfort me." - Psalms 23:1-4

Allow the Lord to turn it around. We all go through struggles; what differentiates you is how you handle them and determine the outcome. This tangible change begins with your internal dialogue, changing your outlook and narrative. Choose to learn the lessons attached to the process; they bring freedom and contentment. Rest is such a powerful weapon; nothing moves you, and you remain calm, able to receive and think clearly.

God desires that you are empowered as you shift your focus from negativity to possibility. Say no to distraction, accusation, or the whispers of that enemy. Celebrate your life, live in victory, and believe in that which is exquisite.

Precious life,
Grant me the resolution
To change what I am capable of changing
And the refinement
To accept what is beyond my control
Help me cherry-pick my conflicts sensibly

Comfort me to repair what is fragmented in my life
Mend and heal every broken sprit
Help me to accept what cannot be reconciled or fixed
Allow me to purge the dead wood accordingly

I desire to disconnect from paths of diminishment
I crave to plug into circuits of extensive improvement
I celebrate and welcome the return of light
I give thanks for the blessing of darkness that...
Now has me so ready to embrace the light

Just as the river cannot flow upstream, I understand that I cannot go back, I brace for the new adventures

Grant me the forte
To fully seize each day
To cherish each moment
Relishing every second that dispenses delight, significance, and satisfaction!

Angels are nondenominational and will help you in whatever spiritual or religious form resonates with you.

Archangel Michael

Archangel Michael is probably the most well-known of the archangels. He is the great protector and the most powerful of the archangels. You can call on Michael when you need protection of any kind. If you are scared or concerned for your safety, Michael will be there to help you. He offers courage and guidance when you feel lost, and he loves to help healers perform their work.

Archangel Rafael

Archangel Raphael assists in physical healing. He is there for you when you are sick, and if you are a healer or work in healthcare, then you can trust that he is always by your side. When it comes to mental health or addiction, Raphael will guide you to clear fear and stress so you can restore your inner peace. He will always lead you towards harmony.

Archangel Gabriel

Archangel Gabriel is a messenger for God and an angel for communications. He helps artists, writers, and teachers share their messages with clarity and meaning. You do not have to be a professional communicator to call on Gabriel. If you are having trouble speaking up or putting something into words, Gabriel will help you find the right way to say it.

Archangel Azrael

Archangel Azrael helps people when they are dying and helps newly crossed-over souls adjust to the spiritual realm. Azrael is also there for you if you are grieving a loss. You can ask him for comfort and strength in your grief. If you help people heal from grief, you can call on Azrael to work with you and protect your energy so that you do not absorb others' emotions. It is important to note that Azrael does not just help with the final transition. If you are going through any change in life, you can call on Azrael for guidance.

Archangel Chamuel

Archangel Chamuel's mission is to help bring peace to the world. You can call on him when you are suffering from anxiety, struggling in a relationship, or having a hard time forgiving someone. Chamuel helps us deal with difficult times and gives us courage when we feel defeated and alone. He is the archangel to call on if you are working through problems in a marriage, healing after a breakup, or want to bring peace to any relationship. Chamuel's presence is significant on a societal scale, too. If you wish to heal division and separation within communities, find common ground, and restore oneness, call Archangel Chamuel.

Your Guardian Angel

We all have a guardian angel devoted to our spiritual growth. Their mission is to serve, guide, and protect you while helping you along your spiritual path. Whereas archangels work with everyone, your guardian angel works exclusively with you. They have unconditional love for you and are always by your side. While they are always available to you, they will not intervene in your life without your free will (or unless there is a life-threatening situation that occurs before it is your time to leave your body). Your guardian angel is always on call. When we feel immense grief or despair, we can sense a presence with us in the low moments of life - even if that sense is very subtle. That feeling is the presence of our guardian angel. But your guardian angel is not just for life's most challenging times. You can call on them anytime you want support and protection.

How to Connect to your Guardian Angel and the Archangels

You can call on as many angels as you wish and as often as you desire. They love to come to your aid. You can call on an archangel or guardian angel with a simple prayer. Your sincere desire to connect is all that is required. For example, you can say, "Thank you, Archangel Michael, for helping me through this scary situation. I welcome your protection and guidance."

There is power in prayer.

Once you pray, God listens.

When you pray, storms abate.

While you, those shut doors fling open.

Immediately, answers come on occasions of prayer.

Sometimes, lessons are dispensed instead of answers, even after years of faithful prayer.

When you get on your knees, you will learn how to rekindle hope in every facet of your life.

Satan knows your name but calls you by your sins. God is still in control. Connect with the real power. God will take care of the mysteries. He will touch you in places where you have been assassinated. He knows the person you would have been, the person you should have been and the person you can be. God is healing and restoring you as you call out to Him; reach out and pray. God, help me not waste my time pounding a wall in desperation to convert it into a door. Lord, teach us to put our faith into perspective.

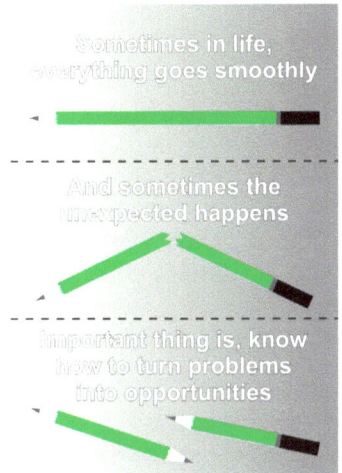

Image 17: You can still be used even if you are broken

"I cry aloud to God, aloud to God, and He will hear me." - Psalm 77:1.

Acknowledgements

As I stand at the culmination of this heartfelt endeavour, I find myself overwhelmed with gratitude and indebtedness to the many individuals and institutions that have supported and guided me throughout the journey of creating this book on suicide prevention and awareness. Their unwavering encouragement, wisdom, and compassion have played an instrumental role in shaping the work that now lies before you. To each one of them, I extend my heartfelt appreciation.

My Family and Friends: My deepest thanks go to my family and friends who stood by me through thick and thin, providing unwavering support, understanding, and love. Your constant encouragement inspired me to delve into the challenging topic of suicide prevention with passion and determination. Thank you for the heartfelt tributes to Jayandra.

Survivors of Suicide Loss: I want to express my profound gratitude to the brave survivors of suicide loss who generously shared their personal stories and experiences with me. Your resilience and willingness to open your hearts have given this book a profound sense of authenticity and empathy.

Research Scholars and Experts: The invaluable insights and groundbreaking research shared by experts in suicide prevention have been an indispensable asset. I thank all the researchers and scholars whose work has informed and shaped the ideas presented within this book.

Health Advocates and Organizations: I acknowledge and appreciate the remarkable work done by various mental health advocacy groups and organizations dedicated to suicide prevention. Your tireless efforts have raised awareness, reduced stigma, and saved countless lives.

Reviewers, Contributors, and Editors: The constructive feedback and meticulous review provided by the dedicated individuals who carefully assessed this manuscript have been invaluable. Your thoughtful edits have undoubtedly enhanced the book's quality and clarity, Cyrene R. To Nadene Joy, your heartfelt foreword will be a balm and an inspiration to many souls. Kudos to you. Azita Abdollahian and Stephanie Cirami, thank you for your valuable book acclaim - gratitude to Jacqueline Wright for her poem. Helen Ena Glen, thank you for sharing your lived experience with your father and PTSD.

Dave Markey: Profound hat tip to you for your impeccable typesetting and graphic design skills. Your talents has added another dimension to this book.

Markey Writing Academy: My sincere gratitude for your unwavering support and dedication throughout the publication process of my book. Kudos to the team, their expertise, guidance and professionalism have been invaluable in bringing this project to fruition. I look forward to continuing our partnership on future endeavors.

Readers and Supporters: Last but not least, I express my sincere gratitude to the readers and supporters of this book. Your interest and commitment to understanding suicide prevention and promoting human welfare are essential to creating a more compassionate and supportive society.

May this book be a small but meaningful contribution to the ongoing effort to prevent suicide and support human welfare. I fervently hope its message will reach those in need and inspire compassion, understanding, and change with profound gratitude.

Thank you, Jayandra, for the delight of sharing life with you and learning so many profound lessons from you, big brother.

About the Author

Kelly Markey is a genuine Renaissance woman, a multifaceted phenomenon. She creates a new pace on every less travelled road; she paves it as she braves it and carves her name in stone. Kelly makes the keyboard hum as a social reformer.

Pursuing the highlights of injustice, Markey has a successful career, including several Nobel prize nominations. She was a finalist for the 2023 Woman Changing the World Award in London. In addition, Kelly was honoured as the Top Executive for the Year 2023 winner by the professional panel at the International Association of Top Professionals in New York. She is the founder and CEO of Markey Writing Academy in Australia.

Buoyed that life has served her with rich and complex experiences, Kelly is a statement of intent with red Porsche confidence. She is a leader and supporter of creating sustainable families and educating children in Uganda. She has a strong partnership with Zululand Lifeline South Africa to improve holistic care and is a member of the Cancer Institute, Australia, to support and champion research. She is an undergraduate of the human spirit and soul.

Kelly Markey exhibits a collision with her optimistic mind, sincere heart, and effervescent elegance, diligently bracing the world with her unparalleled creative prowess. Consequently classy, regularly so regal, and pronounced with ample poise, she carries a spark that not only channelled her path but also ignited the way for many souls. She invokes enlightenment to strive for continuous improvement rather than faking perfection. Markey's writing is compelling and voluptuous, conjuring memories and history of events like a literary godmother. Kelly has the cardinal power to articulate in non-fiction motivation even while gripped in the shadows of suicide.

Kelly's career has been meteoric from corporate professional to blockbuster bestselling and award winning author. Her initial forays into a 'self-help memoir' resulted in what she describes as *'Don't Just Fly, SOAR.'* Her fame as an author is spreading rapidly. Her books have been published in 74 countries to date. In our rhetorical culture, an impeccable wordsmith is skilled at summoning the correct combination of nouns, adjectives, verbs, and taboo topics. Kelly is tagged a Renaissance woman by many platforms for a remarkable reason - an international best-selling author feasting upon her own words. Markey has conquered ample Fujifilm and is a beacon of aspiration in her professional and personal brand. She leaves no doubt that her genius lingers longer than beauty.

Kelly is a paragon success catalyst, born and raised in South Africa, where apartheid coloured her soul, but she refused to let it taint her future. She has travelled to all continents and has citizenship in New Zealand and Australia. She meanders the world and draws inspiration and motivation for writing from our unfair world - her narrative marathons across oceans and dances through great minds. Markey weaves a diverse smorgasbord, and you gain an appreciation for in-depth research. Spellbinding storytelling, emotionally captivated by each case study from start to finish. A grand historian rich in an assortment of ingredients and is a well crafted author.

Kelly strives to live consciously and courageously and relates to others with love and compassion, as she wants to leave this world a better place. She has over 30 years of professional experience as a health executive, including working internationally for major world gorillas in five countries. She has travelled to over 200 cities and has ample experience. She writes from her well-weighed lived experience. She is a philanthropist and supports over 50 charity organisations around the world. She partnered with Zululand Lifeline in South Africa as a long-term partner to enhance humanitarian screams in Africa.

Kelly has inspired and supported thousands of people to navigate their pivotal life moments and champions awareness towards making an excellent brand by transforming your mindset. She consciously works to reduce the trauma and ignorance that surrounds racism and discrimination by prompting healthy conversations that matter. As an international bestselling author, she has appeared on several international media outfits, including several magazine cover features and mainstream television. She has been inundated with requests from a global reader cohort to write more books. Countless people from around the globe have awoken to a vibrantly alive world with a restored life after reading Kelly's debut book, *"Don't Just Fly, SOAR."* She has the advantage of speaking five languages and does fellowship with a broad spectrum of demographics from around the world. She is a confident paragon and exhibits solid boundaries in her professional and personal portfolio.

Kelly writes with enthusiasm and genius for a description that draws you into a captivated world, an exquisite one that bursts from the page and surges into your heart. She lives with her husband on the Central Coast of New South Wales, Australia. She has enthralled avid readers around the world with her expressive pen.

Kelly is a stigma shaker, which she brings to life in her book, *The Life of Jayandra,* by brilliantly compelling suicide reform and prevention. She is, oh, so straightforward - born that way. She shares her exceptional writing skills as she unravels the most painful manuscript she ever had to author. Kelly is the Brand Ambassador of the Global Movement of Hope in Canada. Kelly has resigned from several jobs that paid her substantially because the table did not serve professionalism, integrity, and self-awareness. Her discernment proves that ethics are more important than money in any currency.

Kelly obtained a dual Nobel nomination for her book *Making Sage Decisions*, which was launched in New York City, and this impressive book has taken the world by storm since then. If you want to live your best life, get this book.

Her book *The Life of Jayandra,* won an award for "BOOK of the YEAR 2024" and featured on New York Times Square billboard.

Kelly Markey km
CEO: Markey Writing Academy
Publisher
Writer's Consultant
Global Bestselling Author
Nobel Prize Nominee x 2
Top Executive Award: IAOTP
Women Changing the World Finalist
Brand Ambassador:
Global Movement of Hope
Winner: Book of the Year
Talented Polyglot
kellymarkey.com

Other Books by Kelly Markey

1. Don't Just Fly, SOAR
2. Glean, Grow, and Glow
3. Making Sage Decisions
4. Legacy Playbook
5. Echoes of Humanity – Anthology (Launching October 2024)
6. Lady Diversity Power, Co-author
7. Heart Warrior, Co-author
8. Contentment Unravelled

What Readers Are Saying About Kelly Markey's Books

Magazine Appearances

Markey Writing Academy

Markey Writing Academy is an award-winning company providing impeccable service to bring your expressive pen to life. Kelly's exclusive masterclass is streamlined to offer professional writers a pathway to obtain Nobel nominations and for novice authors to find their voice, affording you impeccable publishing opportunities.

For further information, visit **www.kellymarkey.com**

Work with Kelly Markey

If you are looking to advance your business or personal portfolio:

1. Make Sage Decisions
2. Ambassador of HOPE
3. Craft Resilience
4. Suicide Awareness
5. Navigate Discrimination
6. Business Mentor

I am your Maven!

- Author
- Speaker
- Facilitator
- Subject Matter Expert
- Writers Consultant
- Corporate Advisor
- Publisher
- Website: KellyMarkey.com

Featured On These Top Platforms:

This Book Gives Hope:

Proceeds from the sale of The **Life of Jayandra** go to providing hope to humanity by helping those contemplating suicide at the grassroots level.

It is aligning with Lifeline and suicide prevention globally.

I believe that investing in those who are left to deal with the aftermath of suicide is just as important. Funds will be channelled to help this cohort.

In addition, you can gift this book to your local network, as these pages of compassion and insight will be a beacon of hope for humanity. It will pierce through the darkest seasons with empathy, guidance, and real lived experience.

It offers a lifeline to those in despair, showcasing that even in the depths of anguish, there is a path to resilience, healing, and a brighter tomorrow.

This book is a testament to the power of human connection and the unwavering belief that life can be worth living, no matter how impossible the challenges may seem.

Image 18: Trees of HOPE and GLOOM

Reference

Tributes

1. Tributes to Jayandra from family and friends were published with permission.

2. "Never Lost" was published with permission from poet Jacqueline Wright.

Preface

3. A letter from my friend was incorporated with permission.

Introduction

Chapter 1: Heart to Heart Connection

4. Improving the lives of people with disabilities in South Africa, an Artificial Intelligence source

5. Reference to the theory of human motivation, source ChatGPT, https://chat.openai.com/?model=text-davinci-002-render-sha

6. Image 1: A Theory of Human Motivation by Abraham H. Maslow, edited analysis and specifications by Kelly Markey and CorelDRAW illustration by Dave Markey

7. The reason why dogs are man's best friend is an Artificial Intelligence source

Chapter 2: Unravelling the complexity

8. Image 2: The reality of trusting people with the wrong agenda, analysis and specifications by Kelly Markey and CorelDRAW illustration by Dave Markey

9. Reference to the fire hawk bird, Artificial Intelligence source

10. Image 3: A fire hawk starting a fire on purpose, analysis and specifications by Kelly Markey and CorelDRAW illustration by Dave Markey

11. Why early intervention is significant in preventing suicide, an Artificial Intelligence source

12. Factors to consider when prioritising your welfare, an Artificial Intelligence source

13. Prime Minister Jacinda's reflection, a LinkedIn source

14. Key points on suicide, www.suicideprevention.org

Chapter 3: Human Welfare

15. Meaning of the word seva, the Oxford Dictionary source of reference
16. Nurturing resilience in individuals prone to suicidal thoughts, an Artificial Intelligence source
17. Reference to logotherapy developed by Viktor Frankl, an Artificial Intelligence source
18. Excerpt from my co-authored book, Heart Warrior, Kelly Markey and other authors, Women's Biz Publishing, 2023
19. An excerpt from my colleague's diary was used with permission.
20. Ayurvedic options for depression, https://www.ayurvedagram.com/ayurveda-treatments/treatment-for-depression#:~:text=Ayurvedic%20Medicines&text=1.,which%20helps%20in%20treating%20depression.

Chapter 4: Listening to the Silent Cry

21. Koalas in Australia, an Artificial Intelligence source
22. Paul acknowledges the difficulties Timothy will encounter, The Bible reference source
23. Image 4: disabled hand, analysis and specifications by Kelly Markey and CorelDRAW illustration by Dave Markey
24. The phenomenon known as the attractiveness gap, an Artificial Intelligence source
25. Challenging misconceptions and reducing stigma surrounding suicide, an Artificial Intelligence source

Chapter 5: Suicide Statistics – Let's Change the Narrative

26. Bath, a city in England, the window tax during the 18th and 19th centuries, an Artificial Intelligence source
27. Global Suicide Rates, www.who.org
28. Image 5: graph of suicide statistics, analysis and specifications by Kelly Markey and CorelDRAW illustration by Dave Markey
29. The history of suicide, www.suicideprevention.com
30. Reference to the book *Why People Die by Suicide*, by Thomas Joiner, 2007
31. Changing the narrative around suicide statistics, an Artificial Intelligence source

32. Know the facts on suicide, www.suicideprevention.com

Chapter 6: Kernel of Life

33. Reference to the kernel of life and essence of life, The Oxford Dictionary source of reference

34. The spirit of Ubuntu, an Artificial Intelligence source

35. Image 6: The missing piece, analysis and specifications by Kelly Markey and CorelDRAW illustration by Dave Markey

Chapter 7: Suicide Prevention in the Technology Age

36. Suicide prevention in the digital age, an Artificial Intelligence source

37. Image 7: Data and figure cited as: Ahir, H, N Bloom and D Furceri (2022). "World Uncertainty Index". NBER Working Paper.

38. Reference to the World Uncertainty Index, an Artificial Intelligence source

39. Reference to the Ripple Effect, an Artificial Intelligence source

40. Reference to our environment plays a significant role in shaping narratives, an Artificial Intelligence source

Chapter 8: Residues after Suicide

41. Reference to the kookaburra bird, an Artificial Intelligence source

42. Reference to mourning, an Artificial Intelligence source

43. Image 8: Tips when feeling anxious, analysis and specifications by Kelly Markey and CorelDRAW illustration by Dave Markey

44. Chapter contribution: Effects of PTSD by Helen Ena Glen

Chapter 9: Concepts to Transform Your Life

45. Reference to Phillip Island in Australia, an Artificial Intelligence source

46. Japanese concepts to transform your life, https://betterhumans.pub/7-japanese-concepts-that-will-change-your-life-d750f8d7854

47. Reference to suicidology, https://en.wikipedia.org/wiki/Suicidology#:~:text=Suicidology%20studies%20not%20only%20death,or%20showing%20gestures%20of%20suicide.

48. Reference to the Theory of Change, an Artificial Intelligence source

49. Image 9: Salute to Jayandra, analysis and specifications by Kelly Markey and CorelDRAW illustration by Dave Markey

Chapter 10: What Good Can Spark

50. Reference to Shamwari Game Reserve, https://www.shamwari.com

51. Image 10: What people will REMEMBER, analysis and specifications by Kelly Markey and CorelDRAW illustration by Dave Markey

52. The concept of learn, unlearn, and relearn by Alvin Toffler, https://www.southerncrossinc.com/learn-unlearn-and-relearn/#:~:text=The%20futurist%20and%20philosopher%20Alvin,with%20information%20from%20all%20sides.

53. Suicide of celebrities, https://optimalhappiness.com/celebrity-who-committed-suicide-2/

54. How unbelonging can impact an individual, an Artificial Intelligence source

Chapter 11: Grief and Trauma

55. The difference between trauma and grief, an Artificial Intelligence source

56. How does grief affect the brain, neuroscientist Mary Frances O'Connor, https://www.theguardian.com/science/2022/mar/05/mary-frances-oconnor-the-grieving-brain-grief-psychology

57. Quote from the anthology Heart Warriors, Annie Gibbins and other authors, Women's Biz Publishing, 2023

58. Key aspects of understanding trauma responses, an Artificial Intelligence source

59. Common grief emotions, Rosemary Wanganeen, Griefologist, Clinical Loss and Grief Counsellor-General Public, and EAP provider.

60. Image 11: Photo of Jayandra and Kelly, analysis and specifications by Kelly Markey and CorelDRAW illustration by Dave Markey

Chapter 12: Afterlife and Consciousness

61. What happens when one dies from suicide, an Artificial Intelligence source

62. Nirvana in Buddhism, Artificial Intelligence source

63. Afterlife in Hinduism, an Artificial Intelligence source

64. What does the Bible say about suicide, an Artificial Intelligence source

65. You Start Dying Gradually, written by author Kelly Markey

66. Reference to Hesed Love, an Artificial Intelligence source

Conclusion

67. A Poem to My Brother, written by author Kelly Markey
68. Excerpt from book, Kelly Markey, Heart Warrior, Australia, Women's Biz Publishing, 2023
69. Effective ways to handle and process anger, an Artificial Intelligence source
70. Image 9: The personal alignment, analysis and specifications by Kelly Markey and CorelDRAW illustration by Dave Markey
71. The art of endurance, an Artificial Intelligence source
72. Poem on behalf of Jayandra, written by author Kelly Markey
73. Image 12: Photo of Jayandra captured in 2016 in Sydney, Australia, on a night out for pizza.

Tools to Navigate to a Better Season (Tool1)

74. The Seven Pillars of Empathy, an Artificial Intelligence source

Tips to Build Emotional Resilience (Tool 2)

75. Building emotional resilience and intelligence, https://www.ncbi.nlm.nih.gov/pmc/articles/PMC10132289/

Living YOUR Mission (Tool 3)

76. Image 13: Stages of awareness, analysis, and specifications by Kelly Markey and CorelDRAW illustration by Dave Markey

Anxiety Versus Stress (Tool 4)

77. The distinction between fear and anxiety, an Artificial Intelligence source

The Optimism Gallery (Tool 5)

78. Image 14: Self Love Affirmations, analysis and specifications by Kelly Markey and CorelDRAW illustration by Dave Markey

Mandatory Reporting (Tool 6)

79. Why people may not report suicide, an Artificial Intelligence source
80. Workflow Visio representation, analysis, specifications and illustration by Kelly Markey
81. How to report suicide effectively, an Artificial Intelligence source

Dos and Don'ts of Suicide (Tool 7)

82. Dos and don'ts of suicide, https://www.helpguide.org/articles/grief/

helping-someone-who-is-grieving.htm

Risk Assessment (Tool 8)

83. Risk assessment, www.professionalmanagement.com

84. Image 15: Risk Matrix, analysis and specifications by Kelly Markey and CorelDRAW illustration by Dave Markey

Stop, Start and Continue Matrix (Tool 9)

85. Image 16: Stop, start and continue, analysis and specifications by Kelly Markey and CorelDRAW illustration by Dave Markey

Prayer Pathway (Tool 10)

86. Precious Life poem, written by author Kelly Markey

87. Image 17: You can still be used even if you are broken, analysis and specifications by Kelly Markey and CorelDRAW illustration by Dave Markey

88. Reference to angels, https://gabbybernstein.com/angels/

This Book Gives Hope

89. Image 18: Trees of HOPE and GLOOM, analysis and specifications by Kelly Markey and CorelDRAW illustration by Dave Markey

Kelly Markey

Be The Voice

For Those That Are Too Broken To Raise Their Own

#SuicideAwareness
#SuicidePrevention
#CallOutBadBehaviour

#Hope
#ManagingGrief
#ChangeTheNarrative

www.ingramcontent.com/pod-product-compliance
Lightning Source LLC
Chambersburg PA
CBHW042349300426
44109CB00035B/132